Social Credit for beginners

AN ARMCHAIR GUIDE

BY J.S. OSBORNE & J.T. OSBORNE

PULP PRESS BOOK PUBLISHERS

SOCIAL CREDIT FOR BEGINNERS
COPYRIGHT ©1986 J.S. OSBORNE & J.T. OSBORNE

PUBLISHED BY PULP PRESS BOOK PUBLISHERS
1150 Homer Street
Vancouver Canada V6B 2X6

COVER DESIGN: Thomas Moore
TYPESETTING: Vancouver Desktop Publishing Centre
PRINTING: First Folio Printing Ltd.

*Special thanks to Dona Sturmanis and Calvin Wharton
for their editorial labours.*

CANADIAN CATALOGUING IN PUBLICATION DATA
Osborne, Stephen.
    Social credit for beginners
    ISBN 0-88978-175-3
1. Social Credit. 2. Social credit – Canada –
History. 3. Canada – Politics and government –
20th Century. I. Osborne, Tom, 1949- II. Title
HG355.082   324.271'05   C86-091062-8

PRINTED AND BOUND IN CANADA

This book is dedicated
to the memory of
Greg Enright

CONTENTS

The WORD: England 1919-1939

The VISION: Alberta 1932-1971

The REALITY: British Columbia 1952-19??

AUTHORS' NOTE

In the following pages, we endeavour to outline the broad course of the Social Credit movement since its genesis in England in 1919. It has been an exercise in obscure reading and arcane research—not without its illuminating moments.

Many contemporary observers persist in characterizing Social Credit as a coalition of Liberal and Conservative forces. It is our conclusion that this is an inaccurate perception: we have found in the story of Social Credit the evolution of a political and ethical continuum, the latest stage of which is represented by the Bill Vander Zalm government in British Columbia.

As a political movement Social Credit never achieved worldwide acceptance, but in the course of its evolution it has touched the lives of three generations of British, Canadian and American idealists, intellectuals, crackpots and ordinary people. It is a political reality today for 2 million British Columbians; to millions of others it remains a political anomaly. For a handful of proselytizers, it still holds the potential for earthly salvation.

Our task would have been impossible without the work already done on the subject by the authors listed in the bibliography. Our grateful thanks to them, and to Mary Beth and Dona, for their forbearance.

The WORD

England, 1919-1939

ABC TEA ROOM
LONDON
ENGLAND
1919

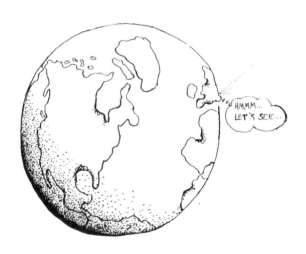

The NEW AGE

Founded 1894, subtitled "A Weekly Record of Christian Culture, Social Service & Literary Life"; espoused "Sweet Reasonableness & Muscular Christianity," then aggressive socialism in 1898. In 1907 it became the leading avantgarde journal in England under A.R. Orage, backed by George Bernard Shaw and others.

The BIRTH of an IDEA

Shortly after the end of World War I, an ex-Army officer began writing essays about money and credit for a leading avant-garde magazine in London, England. The magazine was *The New Age*, devoted to the work of poets and artists as well as some of the leading philosophers of the time. (Its contributors included playwright George Bernard Shaw, historian/novelist H.G. Wells, the American poets Ezra Pound and T.S. Eliot, George Orwell and a myriad of lesser-known luminaries.)

The ex-Army officer was Major C.H. Douglas, a forty-year-old mechanical engineer who, until his appearance in the pages of *The New Age*, had led a life of relative obscurity, untouched by public controversy or political debate. The system of monetary reform and political ethics he was writing about he called Social Credit.

CLIFFORD HUGH DOUGLAS

THE FATHER of SOCIAL CREDIT was born 20 January 1879, in Stockport, England. His father was a draper. Although Douglas claimed Scottish ancestry, there is no record of a Scottish connection. Very little is known of his personal history, early or late. He entered Cambridge University when he was over thirty, and spent only four terms there. Library records indicate that he never borrowed a book.

Douglas was already a mechanical engineer when he entered Cambridge, although how he received his training is unknown. He was a secretive man who became a public figure rather late in life. His public addresses and his writings reveal almost nothing about himself, his wife or his only daughter. His private correspondence appears to have been limited to dinner invitations.

C.H DOUGLAS HERE, BUT MY FRIENDS CALL ME "MAJOR". 'TIS SAID THERE'S NOT MUCH KNOWN ABOUT ME AND THAT I'M "A SOLITARY MAN WHO LIKES SAILING AND FISHING" TO THAT I'D LIKE TO SAY: .... UH.... .... AND ! SO .... WELL....

Douglas had developed a scheme that combined highly unconventional monetary reform with the ethical system known in the nineteenth century as *liberalism*. It appealed most strongly to disaffected elements of the middle class, among whom could be counted (in the 1920s) many members of the Anglo-American avant-garde.

13

Major Douglas, inherently a rather colourless character, never considered himself a member of the avant-garde, but his ideas had made a big impression on the magazine's decidedly colourful editor, A.R. Orage, who took it upon himself to introduce Douglas to the modernist movement.

...BE AS I WAS CONSIDERED BY GEORGE BERNARD SHAW AND T.E. LAWRENCE TO BE A GOOD CRITIC, OF "GRACE AND DISTINCTION", POLITICALLY, I FELT SOCIALISM TO BE ESSENTIALLY AN INTELLECTUAL MATTER. WITH NO ROOM FOR SENTIMENT OR OTHER RELATED WA-WHAH-GOOSH

A.R. ORAGE

ALFRED RICHARD ORAGE was born in 1873 to a farming family in East Anglia. He was educated to be a teacher, but his real interest lay in the art and thought of the emerging avant-garde. He met George Bernard Shaw and G.K. Chesterton in the early years of the century, and with them formed the Leeds Art Club. Later he was secretary to the short-lived Guild Restoration League, a labour reform movement. Not until he assumed editorial control of The New Age did he discover his true calling, and within a couple of years he brought the journal into the forefront of cultural taste. By 1920 his regular contributors included T.E. Lawrence, Max Beerbohm, Patrick Geddes, T.E. Hulme, Cecil Chesterton, G.D.H. Cole, Ezra Pound, Katherine Mansfield, Herbert Read, Hilaire Belloc and, of course, Major C.H. Douglas. He was one of the first to publish Modern Art in England, reproducing the work of Epstein and Picasso, and the sculpture of Gaudier-Brzeska.

Orage was a flamboyant personage in those days: an outspoken "intellectual socialist" (as he called himself) of rather uneven convictions, he opened his pages to a wide range of political and social thought. Hilaire Belloc and Cecil Chesterton, for example, were authoritarian mediaevalists; Herbert Read was an anarchist, and Katherine Mansfield a socialist. After publishing Major Douglas in 1919, Orage became a Social Credit enthusiast, and remained its champion for most of his life—even after he abandoned The New Age in 1922 to join the mystic followers of Gurdjieff and Ouspenski in France.

Orage gave Social Credit its English premiere: without his early support, "Douglasism" might never have emerged as a political or economic movement.

The New Age was nominally a socialist paper, but its pages were open to writers of all political hues: socialists, anarchists, totalitarians, medievalists, individualists, underconsumptionists, and distributists (we'll get to some of these later); when the Major's work first appeared there, it found an audience among all these groups.

For the Major offered something that no one of many schools of thought had been able to offer: an apparently simple solution to the complex economic problems of the twentieth century. Not revolutionary in the usual sense of that word, Douglas's Social Credit scheme was founded on a special understanding of money and credit. Douglas proposed that *credit*, being a reflection of the potential wealth of the nation, should be distributed to the general population as money. By this means poverty would be eliminated without the messy business of taking from the rich to give to the poor.

Douglas' early writings were based on a quasi-mathematical formula derived from his insights into the relationship between *production* and *consumption* (thus side-stepping the Marxist examination of *labour* and *capital*). By the fall of 1919, only a few months after its first appearance in *The New Age*, the A+B Theorem, as the formula came to be known, had become a subject of hot debate among the intelligentsia and was being discussed seriously in political and labour circles. (In October, Douglas was invited to speak to the newly formed National Guilds League. His ideas would prove controversial enough to add to the break-up of that organization into right and left wing factions.)

The ABC Tearoom in High Holborne was a regular meeting place for followers of *The New Age*; in the early '20s the new-fangled Social Credit (also called "Douglasism") was often the main topic of conversation. Monetary theory had rapidly become an issue as volatile as feminism or socialism, and as contentious as Pablo Picasso's Cubism or Wyndham Lewis' Vorticism ...

The '20s was a great time for "isms"—many of them now forgotten. The excitement that surrounded Douglasism we can account for to some extent by attributing it in hindsight to ...

The Historical
FAILURE OF LIBERALISM

The central myth of nineteenth-century liberalism held that individual virtue, determination and effort always find their reward. This is the myth that nourished the emerging entrepreneurial ranks of the middle class for nearly a century of untrammelled "free enterprise" and competition. Its political manifestation was the liberal policy of laissez-faire and free trade; its ideal was an independent small property-owning class consisting of merchants, professionals, farmers and other small businessmen. Its system of private property, profit and competition was quite different from the emerging system of "big business," or capitalism; although ironically, it was the free enterprise system itself that spawned the era of big business.

A Note on Liberalism

Liberalism was the ideology of the emerging middle class created by the industrial revolution. By the beginning of the 20th Century, the liberal position might be defined as follows:

In economics: a belief in laissez-faire "hands-off" free trade, the vitality of small business, opposition to trade unions.

In politics: a demand for minimal government intervention and regulation.

In social ideology: support of equal opportunity for achievement, opposition to aristocracy, and opposition to enforced equality of income.

In culture: anti-clericalism and anti- traditionalism.

(Source: Seymour Lipset, Political Man)

The first Great Depression of our modern age hit the industrial world over a hundred years ago in 1875, and lasted fifteen years. It was a major demonstration of the weakness inherent in the free enterprise system: large corporations whose control of markets and credit was powerful enough began to destroy their smaller competitors, and to align themselves into cartels and monopolies.

Capitalism can be said to have matured during this time. Particularly significant to the future development of Social Credit theory was the consolidation of the banking system. Of the 273 banking companies in England in 1890, only 100 or so remained in 1907. By the end of the First World War there would only be 40 banking institutions left in the country.

CAPITALISM
WAS MATURING . . .

This concentration of power and wealth among the industrialists was met by the growth of a countervailing force among the working classes, who began to organize unions to protect themselves and to improve the conditions of working-class life. By the end of the 1880's, unionism was promising to change the complexion of economic and political philosophy everywhere in the industrial world.

The traditional employer's privilege of bargaining individually with workers was gradually becoming a thing of the past. As the working class organized itself, industrial interests began to clamour noisily for protection (from both labour and foreign competition) and the state began to play an increasing part in the control of economic and social life. Liberal "hands-off" policies were gradually abandoned as the government took an active part in attempting first to destroy, and then to control, organized labour, while mediating between the big international corporations.

In the early part of this century, labour militancy was on the rise everywhere in the West. In England by 1912 the number of production days lost through strikes reached 40 million (from about 5 million in 1907). That year Winston Churchill sent armed troops against workers striking in Liverpool while battleships in the Mersey kept their guns trained on the city.

The independent middle class—comprising small shopkeepers, teachers, preachers, lawyers, doctors, farmers, craftsmen—found itself and its interests increasingly overshadowed by a struggle that at times could be seen to assume epic proportions: the confrontation of organized capital by organized labour.

With the First World War, governments became increasingly active in the daily life of nations; and the modern nation-state began to take form. The old liberalism was on its last legs. (More than half a century later, we can say that it still is.) In place of the ideology of individualism and the system of free enterprise arose ideologies of collectivism and organized interest groups, and systems of large government and administrative bureaucracies.

The era of free enterprise had ushered in the modern age of industrialism; it had created the new urban working class and a class of new poor; it had spawned huge corporate monopolies and an international trade union movement; its work, in a sense, was done. New forces were at play on the historical stage.

By the end of World War I, the middle classes were economically better off than they had been fifty years earlier (in fact, their position on the whole was much improved), but they no longer occupied centre stage. Forced to accept bit parts, they had been pushed into the wings of history by the conflicting forces of industrial capitalism and organized labour. Reacting to a sense of spiritual (rather than economic) dispossession, extremists of the middle-class position would, in the first decades of the century, embrace a variety of political strategies (including fascism and other totalitarian movements) in an attempt to regain the spiritual centre of the age.

A perceived degeneration of British liberalism became a major preoccupation for many intellectuals of the period, some of whom devoted themselves to developing political and economic schemes that might halt the degenerative process, and set the world aright.

Liberal thinkers who clung to ideals of individual freedom were frightened by both the growth of big capitalism and the growth of organized labour. To an "individualist," any form of human organization meant necessarily a loss of free will, and therefore of personal freedom.

The predicament for the individualists was to create a system that would solve the economic problems of the world (essentially, that is, to eliminate poverty) without anyone having to get organized. Faced with this dilemma, a group of individualist economic tinkerers emerged under the general designation of ...

The UNDERCONSUMPTIONISTS

(an ungainly name for a simple idea)

The Underconsumptionists, of which Major Douglas was to become the best known, maintained that modern economies, based on the production of goods and services, were inherently unsound because it was impossible for them to create enough purchasing power to buy all the goods and services they produced, and would be bound to cycles of boom and bust and perpetual poverty for many. Their solution lay in economic systems based on *need*, or consumption. The problem with the present system, they held, lay not in overproduction, as traditional economists usually maintained, but rather in *underconsumption*—the inability of the population to buy the fruits of production. Its solution, they maintained, lay in getting more purchasing power into the hands of more and more people.

The Underconsumptionist dilemma was: how to reform the system without interfering with the (middle-class) individual's "right" to personal autonomy and the pursuit of wealth?

These Individualists were fiercely opposed to the Socialist ideas of the planned economy and the right to economic equality, and they rejected both Liberal and Conservative parties, which they saw as gradually coming under the influence of "creeping socialism" (the bogeyman of the 20th century). During the last decade of the nineteenth century, and right up to the Second World War, individualist thinkers maintained a tradition of anti-socialist (and often anti-capitalist) monetary and economic critique through a proliferation of small groups such as the Free Trade in Capital League (1899) and the Liberty and Property Defense League.

1887 LIBERTY & PROPERTY
DEFENCE LEAGUE
"Reform through Voluntaryism"
("Down with Statism")

Not to Mention the
NATIONAL THRIFT SOCIETY
"A Cheese—paring and
Penurious Attitude"

THE FREE TRADE **1889**
IN CAPITAL LEAGUE
"HANDS OFF THE MIDDLE CLASS"
("No Gov't is Good Gov't")

1905
THE CREDIT REFORM LEAGUE
Arthur Kitson, Prop.
& (Soon to become the
BANKING & CURRENCY
REFORM LEAGUE)

IT'S **NOT** THE WEIGHT YOU UNDERSTAND, BUT WHERE TO **PUT** THE BEGGARS!

Underconsumptionists belong to the "underworld" of economic theory that John Maynard Keynes refers to in his *General Theory.* Individualist thought before World War I culminated with the Banking and Currency Reform League, headed up by Arthur Kitson. Kitson developed some of the early conspiracy theories that Douglas and some of his followers would build on during the period between the wars.

ARTHUR KITSON

THE BLACK SHEEP of a British mercantile family prominent in iron and steel, Arthur Kitson worked with Alexander Graham Bell in Canada. He was a prolific inventor with more than 500 patents, the most important of which was the Kitson Light, used in lighthouses around the world. His fortune was estimated at one time to be £500,000. He lost most of it in bad investments, and spent his last £20,000 developing ideas for currency reform. Kitson emphasized the communal nature of credit that Douglas would take as part of his own theory, and gradually developed some of the early conspiracy theories that would eventually find their way into some Social Credit positions. In particular, Kitson laid the blame for the present state of affairs on the doorstep of a German-Jewish conspiracy to enslave the world (the Bolsheviks wouldn't be included until after 1919).

Apparently unaware of the "economic underworld" and its traditions until he began to generate a correspondence in the pages of *The New Age* (a few years later he would acknowledge his predecessors), Major Douglas, apparently on his own, developed an underconsumptionist critique of industrial society, the basis of which he said came to him in a dream ...

The Birth of an Underconsumptionist

One night in darkest England during World War I, Major Douglas, then an obscure Army engineer, lay tucked in his narrow officer-issue cot, dreaming that he was in an enormous hall filled with rows of unattended tabulating machines. The machines (much like the ones he was using to straighten out a bookkeeping problem at Farnsworth Aircraft Works) were clattering away on their own, pouring forth endless rivers of little cards, upon which were neat little columns of numbers.

E-GAD.

"THE NUMBERS ON THE LITTLE CARDS REPRESENTED SOMETHING: WAGES AND SALARIES PERHAPS. WHEN I REALIZED THIS, I BECAME AWARE OF SOMETHING THAT HAD BEEN ONLY VAGUELY BOTHERING ME UNTIL THIS POINT..."

I realized precisely this: the total of salaries, wages and dividends paid out in a factory in, say, a particular week, never equalled the price of the goods produced in that week. Because the price charged for goods and services is always more than the wages and profits paid in creating them.

This insight led him directly to an underconsumptionist corollary: the country as a whole would never be able to generate enough personal income to buy the whole production of the country.

In other words, total consumption can never equal total production.

The few times that Major Douglas spoke publicly about his dream, he connected it loosely to a few anecdotes taken from his own life. Each illustrated an economic anomaly that had been bothering him.

A couple of these stories were from a time before the war when he had been employed briefly in India, surveying water resources for Westinghouse. Having determined that there was an abundance of potential hydroelectric power in the survey area, he was told by his superiors that there was no money available to pay for the machinery needed to develop it. But as the water resource itself represented a kind of wealth, and there were apparently plenty of machines available in England with no buyers, it seemed irrational to the Major that development could not ensue.

He tried to discuss the problem over dinner with the controller-general of India, who apparently went on at some length about something he called *credit* before complaining that British Treasury officials persisted in melting down and re-coining rupees because they believed erroneously in something called "the quantity theory of money." Then the controller said, "Of course, silver and gold have nothing to do with the situation."

Immediately before the war, Douglas was working for the Post Office railway. All the machinery and all the labour necessary to get the job done were available; but a shortage of money led to frequent work stoppages and layoffs. But once the war began, there suddenly appeared to be no shortage of money whatsoever, and the work proceeded without a break.

And then, during the war, only a few months before the dream of the tabulating machines ...

I met a member of the Sassoon banking family in France. This gentleman confided in me that *financially speaking, the war could go on forever.*

Always reticent when it came to speaking of himself, Major Douglas never explained in detail how he connected these disparate incidents with the dream he had at Farnsworth; but within a month of the war's end, he was writing about economics and the monetary system in an engineering journal; and two months later A.R. Orage was publishing him in *The New Age*.

When Douglas appeared among the fringe economists of the early '20s, he found an attentive audience among moderate socialists and right-wing liberals as well as avant-garde poets and artists. This was not a large audience, and it was not a cohesive one; but from it grew a small body of disciples whose proselytizing would keep Social Credit ideas alive longer than any others to emerge from the world of underground economics. During this time his lectures drew the curious, the thoughtful, and often the eccentric.

"UNDERCONSUMPTIONIST COROLLARY": "the country as a whole would never be able to generate enough personal income to buy the whole production of the country."

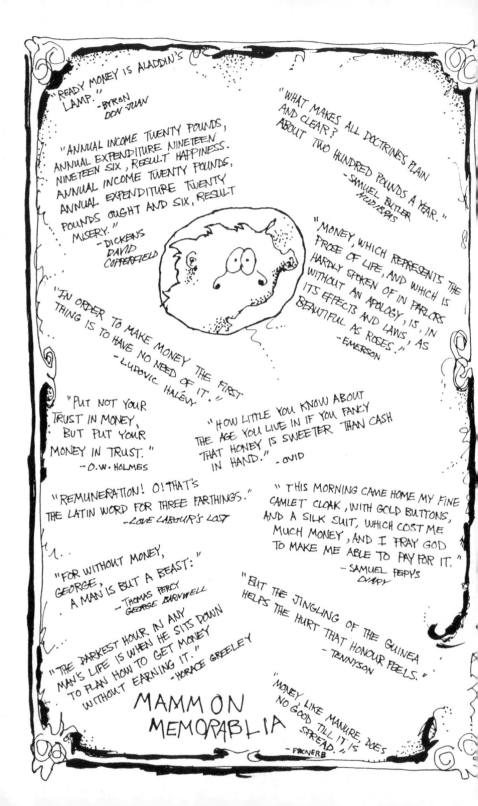

"READY MONEY IS ALADDIN'S LAMP."
—BYRON
DON JUAN

"WHAT MAKES ALL DOCTRINES PLAIN AND CLEAR? ABOUT TWO HUNDRED POUNDS A YEAR."
—SAMUEL BUTLER
HUDIBRAS

"ANNUAL INCOME TWENTY POUNDS, ANNUAL EXPENDITURE NINETEEN NINETEEN SIX, RESULT HAPPINESS. ANNUAL INCOME TWENTY POUNDS, ANNUAL EXPENDITURE TWENTY POUNDS OUGHT AND SIX, RESULT MISERY."
—DICKENS
DAVID COPPERFIELD

"MONEY, WHICH REPRESENTS THE PROSE OF LIFE, AND WHICH IS HARDLY SPOKEN OF IN PARLORS WITHOUT AN APOLOGY, IS, IN ITS EFFECTS AND LAWS, AS BEAUTIFUL AS ROSES."
—EMERSON

"IN ORDER TO MAKE MONEY THE FIRST THING IS TO HAVE NO NEED OF IT."
—LUDOVIC HALÉVY

"PUT NOT YOUR TRUST IN MONEY, BUT PUT YOUR MONEY IN TRUST."
—O.W. HOLMES

"HOW LITTLE YOU KNOW ABOUT THE AGE YOU LIVE IN IF YOU FANCY THAT HONEY IS SWEETER THAN CASH IN HAND."
—OVID

"REMUNERATION! O! THAT'S THE LATIN WORD FOR THREE FARTHINGS."
—LOVE LABOUR'S LOST

"THIS MORNING CAME HOME MY FINE CAMLET CLOAK, WITH GOLD BUTTONS, AND A SILK SUIT, WHICH COST ME MUCH MONEY, AND I PRAY GOD TO MAKE ME ABLE TO PAY FOR IT."
—SAMUEL PEPYS
DIARY

"FOR WITHOUT MONEY, GEORGE, A MAN IS BUT A BEAST:"
—THOMAS PERCY
GEORGE BARNWELL

"THE DARKEST HOUR IN ANY MAN'S LIFE IS WHEN HE SITS DOWN TO PLAN HOW TO GET MONEY WITHOUT EARNING IT."
—HORACE GREELEY

"BUT THE JINGLING OF THE GUINEA HELPS THE HURT THAT HONOUR FEELS."
—TENNYSON

MAMMON
MEMORABLIA

"MONEY, LIKE MANURE, DOES NO GOOD TILL IT IS SPREAD."
—PROVERB

A BRIEF HISTORY
of MONEY AND CREDIT
with Major C.H. Douglas

Now, to begin at the beginning: the first money systems were little more than barter systems, because the medium of exchange was valuable in itself. In hunting societies, skins might have exchange value; in a pastoral cultures bushels of grain or herd stock were used as a kind of money. Later in the evolution of our culture, a wide variety of valuable things served also as exchange mediums: tea, corn, olive oil, coconuts. New England colonists used tobacco as money. The metal disks of gold or silver which we tend to think of as money had an intrinsic value as precious metals, but did not have the use value that skins or a pair of oxen might provide the recipient.

But from a very early date it was apparent to some people— forerunners of today's bankers—that money itself need not have any substantial value in order to be used as a medium of exchange. Even the early brass and copper coins derived their value not only from their metallic content, but as well from the mere fact that they were *used* as money—we can say that they had been monetized. It follows that anything could be monetized in this way: by simply using it as an exchange medium.

A piece of paper has little value in itself; but when monetized, it becomes valuable. This was realized as long ago as the thirteenth century, when Kublai Khan issued a paper currency.

In England, credit money was first used by the goldsmiths. They received gold from depositors, against which they issued receipts. These receipts were more convenient than gold, and circulated freely as money. Here we see the origin of both the modern bank note and the bank cheque.

Goldsmiths soon came to realize that they could safely issue more receipts—and circulate them as money—than they had gold with which to back them. Just so long as everyone didn't try to cash them in at the same time. These people were the first modern bankers, having created a new form of money: paper notes issued solely on the credit of the issuing goldsmith.

When the Bank of England came into existence in 1694, this practice of issuing tickets against non-existent gold became institutionalized as the reserve system of banking. It is essentially the system we have today. The bank maintains a certain reserve of gold against which it issues paper notes far in excess of the amount of gold in the reserve.

This way, the banking system builds an inverted pyramid of credit on an apex of gold. All goes well until too many people cash in their notes at the same time, and the whole thing crashes to the ground. The notion that our money is based on a supply of gold is a fiction. People continue to accept paper money not for its intrinsic value—that is, its value as paper—or for the gold it might be said to represent, but simply because they believe in its effectiveness to buy. That's what gives it value.

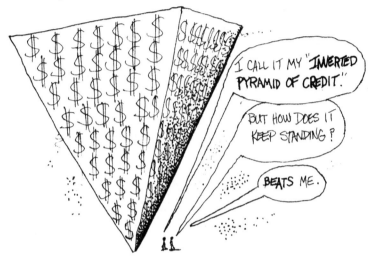

Modern money can be defined simply as "a claim on goods and services," or more succinctly, as "tickets," which have little or no value in themselves. It is any medium which has reached such a degree of acceptability that no matter what it is made of, no one will refuse it in exchange for products or service.

But in fact, money in the form of currency—coins, bank notes, treasury notes, etc.—is only used in about 10% of all transactions. At least 90% of our transactions use money in the form of bank deposits, which are transfered by means of bank cheques. There is far less *currency* in circulation than there is *money* at our command. Increasing or decreasing the amount of currency has very little effect on the total amount of money.

So far so good. The Major begins to develop what we can recognize as Social Credit when he gets to the question of how money is created ...

Many people think bank deposits represent real money placed in a vault for safe-keeping. But in fact, most bank *deposits are created by loans the banks themselves make.* When we borrow from a bank,

31

an account is opened in our name and we are allowed to draw against the amount of the loan. This deposit represents money that didn't exist before the loan was made! Even individual cash deposits are only the redeposit of deposits which originated somewhere along the line in loans.

Every bank loan *creates* money and every *repayment* of a bank loan *destroys* money! For example, when a banker lends £100,000 to a manufacturer, he writes that number in a ledger, creating a brand new deposit. The banker doesn't take money out of someone else's deposit and put in the new one. The manufacturer can then draw on that deposit any sum up to the £100,000.

When the borrower write a cheque, that amount of the cheque represents money to him and to the community. But most importantly: it is *new* money that didn't exist before, an addition to the community's stock of money, quite simply because that new deposit does not lessen the amount of any other deposit.

Even if the loan is secured by collateral, it still represents new money. Security in the form of stocks, bonds, mortgages etc, are not drawn upon in any way for the creation of that £100,000. They remain unaffected by the new money, even though they might be locked up in the bank's vault.

Now, why does the banker create this money, and make such a loan? To make a profit, of course. The banker believes that the borrower will repay the money within a certain time, and also pay interest on that money.

So what convinces the banker that the borrower will be able to repay the loan? Simply this: aside from collateral security (which is really a kind of insurance for the banker—not something he wants to own), the real basis of such a loan is the banker's belief that the manufacturer will produce a commodity (or service) that consumers will want to consume—and that enough consumers will be able to consume enough of the product to enable the producer to pay back the bank, with the interest.

In other words, if the banker didn't believe in the ability of the community at large to *produce and consume*, he would never make the loan. It is upon the strength of the community's capacity to produce, deliver and consume goods and services that bank loans are created.

The source of all credit, then, is in the ability of the community to produce and deliver goods and services as, when and where required. And that's the nub of it.

According to Major Douglas:

The real wealth of a community is that thing the banker has to believe in, in order to create the loan: the community's ability to produce and deliver goods and services where and when they are required. And further, the real credit of the community is that very belief in the ability of the community to produce, deliver and consume.

Real Credit is a possession of the community.

Financial Credit is merely an expression of Real Credit in monetary form.

33

Wealth lies not in money itself. *Money is nothing.* You cannot eat it, wear it, or get out of the rain under it. It is only of use if there are goods and services available for which it may be exchanged. A bag of gold in the desert is not wealth.

The bank loan is made against the Real Credit of the community. It takes the form of Financial Credit, which is merely a monetary expression of that real credit. By controlling financial credit for its own profit, the banking system has control of the Real, or *Social Credit* that belongs in the first place to the community at large, and would not exist at all without the community.

It is patently absurd that the banks should charge the community for the use of its own credit.

To Douglas, the evils of modern life grew out of an irrational monetary system caught up in the spiralling effect of bank loans. As producers endeavour to sell their products they are forced to persist in the cycle of borrowing new money to pay old debts, in anticipation of a day when there might be enough purchasing power (in the form of wages, salaries and dividends) in the community to actually buy those products.

Such a day is never to come under the present system. For, as Douglas realized during the war, the purchasing power created by the present system will *never* be enough to buy all of the production of the system.

He worked this insight into a crude formula that became the basis of Social Credit monetary theory:

THE A + B THEOREM

The price of goods and services consists of two parts:

A : Wages, salaries and dividends. These are paid to individuals.

B : Raw materials, bank charges and other external expenses. These are paid out to other organizations.

The price of all goods and services, then, is the sum of A + B. But the purchasing power created by those prices consists only of A. It follows then, that the public will never be able to buy all the goods and services produced.

The question, then, is how are the B payments made? They must be coming from somewhere, or the system would collapse.

Douglas proposed that the B payments were being made in the form of credit. Banks, by extending credit to the manufacturers, were creating the new money needed for the B payments. It was Douglas' contention that the banks had no right to this control over credit; and that it was through this control that they maintained the general population in a position of servility.

(Students of economic theory will recognize in the A + B Theorem echoes of Karl Marx's theory of Surplus Value. For a good explanation, see *Marx for Beginners*, Writers and Readers, London)

Banks control the credit that Douglas claimed belongs to the community; he wanted to put that credit in the hands of the public.

He proposed to do this by developing a central accounting agency that would keep track of all the potential and real value in the country's resources, and issue money to the public in proportion to that evaluation in the form of National Dividends (we'll get to them later). This agency would also control prices and eliminate profiteering.

Much of the Douglas critique of the modern money system made sense in the '20s and still does. He could point to it as a system kept more or less intact by a complex network of bank loans, foreign market development, wars and industrial sabotage.

Then, as now, what he termed "industrial sabotage" was not uncommon: tons of coffee dumped into the sea, acres of wheat burned off, farmers paid not to grow crops, livestock killed off—all to keep prices high among those with money. And this when millions of people are starving.

Douglas characterized nations seeking foreign trade as trying "desperately to supplement their own inadequate purchasing power by exchanging goods for money." In order to obtain a favourable balance of trade, "it is not uncommon for one nation to supply another with the money necessary to buy its goods."

> It is this frenzied struggle among nations to recover abroad the money that does not exist as purchasing power at home that leads inevitably to war.

Douglas claimed that, finally, it is production during war that serves temporarily to lessen the discrepancy between production and consumption that he summarized in the A+B Theorem. By expanding production into the area of war materials, which are of no consumable value to the community, more wages, salaries and dividends (A payments) are distributed throughout the community, thereby increasing purchasing power without increasing the supply of consumer goods.

Although the community as such has no need of bombs, guns, airplanes, etc, it does receive money during the course of their production—money that can be applied to consumable goods during the same period. The more ammunition used up, the more planes that crash, the more men that are killed, the more money flows into consumers' pockets. The State pays the bill, of course, by borrowing money from the banks, who make their profits in the form of interest. And the community will be paying forever for the temporary prosperity it experiences in times of war.

Douglas maintained (with some reason, as we can see from his analysis of money) that war itself keeps our economic system operating. But further than that, and not so reasonably, he claimed that the wars of the modern world, and its attendant economic ills, were the result of an active conspiracy: as early as 1922 he was writing about "the existence of great secret organizations bent on the acquisition of world empire."

This belief in "great secret organizations" is the paranoid root of the Social Credit movement (as it is of other extreme forms of middle-class revolt); in it we hear a note of irrationality ringing inside a system of thought that claimed above all others to be rationally conceived and scientifically developed.

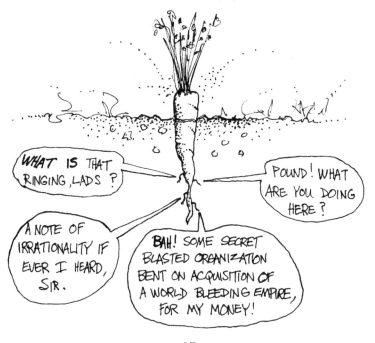

37

An IDEA TAKES ROOT

After 1919 Douglas committed himself to articulating a system of monetary techniques he and his followers believed would rid the world of the evils of capitalism and collectivism (that is, Big Business and Organized Labour) while restoring the middle class virtues of individual initiative and free, small-scale enterprise.

That system, as illuminated by the Major and his followers in dozens of books and hundred of articles, is not easy to grasp in all its detail: observers have frequently characterized it as incomprehensible in those areas where it is not merely obscure; even the Alberta government (the only one in the world to attempt enactment of the scheme) would admit to an imperfect understanding of it, and be forced to look in vain for "expert" help from England.

But even in its complexity, Douglas's plan excited the imaginations of many thinkers both left and right. The A+B Theorem and Douglas's definition of Real Credit offered a quick fix to economic problems; for a while at least, Social Credit seemed to offer a new kind of reality.

The first political organization to entertain Douglas's ideas was the National Guilds League, which invited him to speak in late 1919 and again in December 1920—this second meeting to consider adopting Social Credit as League doctrine.

The National Guilds League had emerged from the pre-World War I labour movement which developed the General Strike as its most powerful weapon in the struggle for workers' rights. Guild socialists advocated the organization of workers into autonomous guilds which would control production in each sector of industry. The guilds would administer to the well-being of their members, and coordinate their efforts through a central parliament. It was essentially a decentralized form of socialism, and attracted a wide range of support from socialists, anarchists, labour leaders and even Anglican Bishop William Temple, later to become Archbishop of Canterbury. By 1917, the largest unions in the country—miners, railway workers and postal workers—had all come out for some form of Guild Socialism.

Guild Socialism offered a decentralized alternative to State Socialism, and for this reason appealed ethically to reformers afraid of centralized government; at the same time its economic theory appealed to Marxist thinkers. As such, it was an uneasy compromise, unable to hold itself together as a movement after the success of the Bolsheviks in the Russian Revolution.

In 1919, the movement split on the question of supporting the Bolsheviks, with the radicals going over to the newly formed Communist Party of Great Britain. The moderate reformers, left with half a movement, and no viable program of action, saw in Social Credit a ready-made alternative to the evils of "Big Socialism."

Douglas's ideas found a powerful supporter in the Guilds League secretary, Maurice Reckitt, and an equally powerful opponent in G.D.H Cole, an Oxford don and respected Socialist writer. Cole perceived from the outset that Social Credit was fundamentally in contradiction to the Guild Socialists, who maintained that the first step toward reform lay in the control of *production*—and not,as the Douglasites maintained, in the distribution of purchasing power to the consumer. But Reckitt drew many supporters, and the debate of December 1919 was a stormy one, ending nevertheless in the defeat of the Social Credit initiative, and later the collapse of the Guild Socialist Movement. Douglas was attacked on various grounds: by some for his emphasis on currency reform; and by other more orthodox socialists who felt that financiers depended just as much on workers as workers did on them. One of these, S.G. Hobson, said: "This is the first time I've heard of an ethical proposition coming out of a mathematical formula. I suggest that Bertrand Russell be informed of this." The vote was 41 to 13 against Social Credit.

But new converts to Social Credit within the League were not about to give up: several factions broke away in protest to set up Social Credit study groups, and by the end of 1921 there were about forty cells of Douglasites scattered over the country.

Major Douglas was bitterly disappointed by the League's rejection of his scheme, as were some of his closest followers, including A.R. Orage. It was, after all, understandably difficult for them to accept repudiation of a scheme that claimed to be a mathematically demonstrable solution to all of the world's problems. As Douglas wrote of it later, "I had the idea that I had got hold of some very specific technical information and I had only to get it accepted; I had the idea that I had only to run to father and he would be very pleased about it."

The Guild Socialists turned down a program of monetary reform grounded in an ethical system held in suspicion by most of them. That ethical system was old-fashioned Liberalism; Douglas's program of monetary reform was perceived to be its idealistic superstructure.

The Social Credit scheme rejected by the League was in fact an expert system. Douglas claimed that this was its major administrative strength: once implemented, it would be tended by hired experts trained to operate it like a machine; the citizenry would reap its benefits, and never have to worry about how it worked . .

THE GIST OF IT, or

A Brief Look at (some of) the Details

Douglas based his scheme of Social Credit on three concepts:

The Cultural Heritage
The National Dividend
&
The Just Price

First, then, the Cultural Heritage:

The Cultural Heritage, according to Douglas, was the basis of the nation's Real Credit: the totality of the capital and human assets of the nation. This was what the banker had to believe in before he would make the loan.

(Our Real Credit, you will remember, has been appropriated by the bankers, who dispense it only to generate profits for themselves.)

The Major proposed to distribute a portion of the Cultural Heritage to the general public by means of payments he called The National Dividend. In this way the public would gain purchasing power outside the usual channels of industry, which, under the present system, distribute most of the consumer's money in the form of wages, salaries and dividends.

This is where the "experts" enter the picture. Functionaries working for a National Credit Authority would be charged with the task of discerning the Real Credit of the nation, and dispensing it to the citizenry by regular direct payment:

The National Credit Authority would be an army of bookkeepers, endlessly perusing tables of statistics, manufacturer's balance sheets, actuarial tables, Labour Board statistics, the census, income taxes, unemployment figures, etc ...

The size of the National Dividend would be computed on a regular basis:

> Let us presume the country's production capacity to be 100 units, and
> its ability to consume only 40 units. This leaves a 60 unit disparity
> between Real Credit and Financial Credit. In such a case, the govern-
> ment would issue credit to the public to the extent of that remaining
> 60 units.

The National Dividend would be paid out to every citizen, employed or not. Douglas believed unemployment to be a necessary condition of our modern industrial age; its increase, in an efficiently-run a sign of healthiness. Why should everyone have to work, if all our needs can be met with only some working, and machines doing the rest?

Douglas believed in the Age of Leisure:

The National Dividend would eliminate the need for welfare or unemployment insurance, which are conventionally paid for through taxation. In the Social Credit state, no one would be taxed to assist the less fortunate. (In a free enterprise society, there exists no obligation between "free" individuals.) But the Dividend would go to everyone, even those who didn't want to work:

Others who wished to better themselves through various forms of employment would be encouraged to work and contribute in that way to the national wealth. Fewer people would be forced into jobs for which they have no ability or inclination:

44

But the National Credit Authority would have more to do than merely distribute the National Dividend. Just as the Major proposed that there is a difference between Financial Credit and Real Credit, he also proposed that there is a difference between the Financial Cost of a product or service and its Real Cost.

The Real Cost of production lies only in consumption, that is the total amount of energy and materials consumed in its making. Consider for instance, the making of a violin: the destruction of timber, the wear and tear of tools and machinery, the food, clothing and shelter used by those engaged in making the violin—these are all the physical costs attached to its manufacture.

The Financial Cost includes capital costs and interest. However, if

45

consumers were charged only the Real Costs they would have sufficient purchasing power to claim the product of industry, because
these are the current costs that have been distributed to the community as wages. At the same time producers would have no trouble
selling their goods.

The NCA would also be in charge of setting prices. The Just
Price of a good or service the Major defined as the Real Cost of its
production; it was to be calculated as the fraction of the Financial
Price corresponding to the ratio of Total National Consumption to
Total National Production. (Is that perfectly clear?)

That ratio is usually about 4 to 1. So under a Just Price system,
anyone buying a pair of shoes priced at $4, a rail ticket priced at
$40, or an automobile priced at $4000, would pay respectively $1,
$10, and $1000. To quote the Major:

> This will of course leave the retailer out of pocket for everything sold.
>
> Under Social Credit, the retailer would be reimbursed through the
> National Credit Account for the money lost on such a discount.
>
> To defeat those few retailers who might raise their prices so high as
> to guarantee themselves huge profits once the discount is paid back
> to them, it would be necessary for anyone dealing with the discount
> to accept the limits of fair or fixed profits, also to be established by
> the National Credit Authority.

The Major claimed that putting his proposals into effect would
not eliminate competition in industry, but would eliminate price-
fixing. Taking the Real Cost as the basis of a fair price—and not
the current level of inflation or deflation—prices would vary only
according to the variety of commodity sold. The retailer who took
advantage of the Just Price Discount would obviously be able to
undersell those who preferred not to make use of it. The principle
of "free choice" is preserved.

(No one said this was going to be easy to understand.):

> The Just Price would vary with the fluctuating ratio of Total National
> Consumption to Total National Production. If at some time in the
> future all direct consumption, plus depreciation of capital wealth, plus
> exports, over a specified accounting period, exactly equalled all pro-
> duction, plus appreciation of capital wealth, plus imports, there would
> be no need for the discount.

So, periodic adjustment of the Just Price would be another
important task of the National Credit Agency.

The Just Price would be calculated from statistics gathered in a previous accounting period, and would be published, say, quarterly. From the public balance sheet, the man in the street would gain accurate knowledge of the degree of his country's prosperity. When prices were high he would know that the wealth of the nation had not increased during the period as much as it had been decreased by consumption. And vice-versa.

The net result* of these innovations would be (according to the Major) a debt-free society that distributed its wealth on a rational basis through the national credit scheme to its citizens. Individual initiative is preserved and encouraged: everyone is free to do as they please, in ...

A Free Enterprise Society
Under Social Credit

---

*Traditional economists attacked Douglas's scheme as being inflationary. Their arguments, however, are beyond the scope of this book. Douglas maintained that the combination of the Just Price and the National Dividend were anti-inflationary: "New money created by the National Credit Account is issued only after prices have been lowered through the retail discount. Therefore it cannot be accompanied by an inflationary increase in prices. The new money is issued only at the point of sale. Not until the retail sale is made is a penny of credit issued."

Douglas clothed the ethical structure of Free Enterprise in a system of monetary and credit reforms that were the distinctive markings of Social Credit theory for the next fifteen years.

At the heart of Free Enterprise is the special notion of freedom of the individual. This private freedom is the Holy Grail of the Free Enterpriser.

In a free enterprise system, people are not perceived to be equal; they are, however, perceived to be equally free. Equally free to do as they please. Free to work, or free to remain idle. It follows, somewhat illogically, that anyone who works does so by choice; anyone who doesn't work is unemployed by choice.

By free choice, individuals achieve their stations in life voluntarily and are responsible for their own well-being.

Free enterprise posits no legitimate obligation to exist between individuals unless entered into by mutual agreement. No one is responsible for anyone else.

Anything that tends to thwart the exercise of this private freedom is perceived to menace it. Large organizations in particular are seen in this threatening light: trade unions, political parties, unemployed workers' organizations, special interest groups of any kind. Within these groups, and others like them, the private freedom of the individual is seen to be crippled; to the free-enterpriser, large groups are merely the tools of the "powermongers" who lead them.

Free enterprisers are deeply suspicious of parliamentary democracy; organized political parties, representing competing interests, are understood to be inimical to the freedom of the "little man." Furthermore, democratic societies tend gradually to increase the equality of different classes and groups: this tendency, in free enterprise eyes, is tyrannical, robbing individuals of their very singularity and "freedom."

The mechanism of monetary reforms proposed by Douglas would put an end to the tyranny of special interests which he saw as the source of all oppression; the combination of the Just Price and the National Dividend would give workers the freedom to refuse low wages, while ensuring employers the right to offer low wages. Trade unions would become unnecessary.

Government would be reduced under Social Credit to the administrative functions of keeping the peace and managing the National Credit Authority.

Parliamentary democracy would be replaced by "Democracy of the Common Will," a concept that Douglas never clarified, except to offer it as a desirable alternative to what he called "democracy of the Intellect or the Emotions."

Social Credit did not mean an end to the class system; nor did it mean an end to exploitation or the dominance of men over women (or any group over any other group). With the Social Credit instrument in place, one's status in society would become one's own responsibility and no one else's.

Society's ills, however, would be expected to fade away of themselves; the Social Credit formula would eliminate the only means by which Douglasites maintain that people gain power over other people: through control of Real Credit.

In the free enterprise utopia that Social Credit offered, small business would thrive and profits would be "reasonable"; working people would contract freely with employers for low wages; those who chose not to work in the world of industry or business would be free to contribute to the Cultural Heritage as they saw fit.

As a system it would exist outside of historical time, oblivious to class structure and wilfully ignorant of the social and political forces shaping the modern world. Social Credit evolved in reaction to modern history, a stubborn Utopian vision of a world of small businessmen and their families.

Douglas worked out the basics of his Social Credit ideas in eleven months. Many of the 32 years remaining to him he would devote to a study of why his scheme seemed doomed never to win widescale acceptance in his own country. From this intense study developed what historian John Finlay has generously characterized as Douglas's "bold analysis of human nature and human motivation ... the identification of the power complex." Which brings us to the last bulwark of Social Credit theory:

The
Pyramid of
POWER

The Major never achieved a systematic analysis of the modern world —as Karl Marx, working from a different hypothesis, can be said to have done. Satisfied that his analysis of money and credit revealed the fundamental workings of modern society, Douglas saw no reason to widen the field of his scrutiny. Instead, he narrowed it down.

"DOUGLAS'S WALK IS THAT OF A PARANOIC." (THE WORLD SHOULD KNOW)...

JOVE! WHAT'S THE BIG IDEA?

DR. JAMES YOUNG (favorite pupil of Jung)

Having established theoretically the natural right of the people to share in the Cultural Heritage and to partake of the Social Credit, Douglas postulated an active conspiracy of bankers, financiers, Jews, communists and Freemasons bent on enslaving the world through manipulation of credit. Over the years he would become obsessed with secret organizations (the existence of which can never be demonstrated, of course, because they're secret) and by the late '30s would even be writing seriously about the *Protocols of Zion*–a document proven by scholars to be a forgery (but accepted by the Nazis as justification for their anti-semitic program), purporting to outline a Jewish conspiracy.

Looking for a Home ...

Defeated at the National Guilds League Meeting, but somehow not disheartened, Social Credit continued to look for a home among organized political groups and the government of the day. A.R. Orage did his best to arrange a meeting between Douglas and the Ministry of Reconstruction. Turned down, he tried to set Douglas up with Lloyd George, the Liberal Prime Minister. Again, no luck.

And then, incredibly, the British Labour Party, intrigued by the "Social Credit question," struck a committee to study Douglasism, and for a time Douglas and Orage thought their best hope might lie with organized labour. This made complete sense to Douglas, who characterized his system as one that anyone should be capable of initiating. It never occurred to him or to Orage that the industrial working class might not find the solution to all its problems in Social Credit .

As Douglas put it: "the labour movement should be the first and most influential supporter of the claim to the social dividend."

But the Labour Party, looking for parliamentary credibility, and afraid to be associated with "radical" ideas either communist or non-communist, eventually rejected Social Credit in a couple of mildly-reasoned postion papers, and hoped that it would quietly disappear.

For a time the Social Credit movement floundered, with no arena other than the pages of *The New Age.* When Orage deserted the paper in 1922 to take up the life of a Gurdjieff-inspired mystic, it even lost that forum for the year of his successor's tenure as editor, a Major Williams, who simply ignored Douglas and his followers. Then in June 1923, Arthur Brenton, a confirmed Douglasite, took over the magazine and opened its pages to contributors from the many tiny study groups around the country.

But without Orage at the helm of *The New Age,* public discussion of Douglasism lacked direction, and for a year the magazine was filled with contradictory interpretations of Social Credit and proposals for its implementation. Some writers criticized *The New Age* for directing its appeal to the middle classes and the intelligentsia, and called for a stronger "language of the pothouse" (presumably to attract the working class); others defended Douglasism as too intellectual for popularizing, and too easily perverted by lowering the level of the discussion. Shared by all sides was a general perception that the existing economic system was in the process of breaking down, and that something must be done soon.

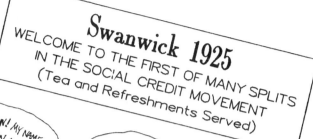

Swanwick 1925

WELCOME TO THE FIRST OF MANY SPLITS IN THE SOCIAL CREDIT MOVEMENT
(Tea and Refreshments Served)

HELLO AGAIN! MY NAME IS ARTHUR KITSON AND ME AND SOME OF THE CHAPS HAVE HAD ENOUGH OF DOUGLAS AND HIS ROT!

WE ARE OBLIGED, THEREFORE, TO FORM THE "ECONOMIC FREEDOM LEAGUE"! THERE ARE TWO REASONS FOR THIS YOU UNDERSTAND — FIRST: YOU OTHER CHAPS INSIST ON FOLLOWING THE MAJOR'S THEORIES TO A "T" AND ARE OPPOSED TO CENTRALIZATION! SECOND: WE'RE HAVING ONE HELL OF A TIME FOLLOWING THAT BEASTLY "A + B THEOREM" OF HIS!

HEAR! HEAR! AND I'M HEB. LUDLOW...

...AND I'M GOING TO EDIT OUR NEW JOURNAL, "THE AGE OF PLENTY" (WHICH WILL BE A DAMN SIGHT BETTER THAN THAT ARTSY-FARTSY "NEW AGE"!)

LATER, I WILL BEGIN TO SHOW A STRAIN OF "MENTAL IMBALANCE"...

...AND ADD THE SUBTITLE: "THE MIGHTY ATOM OF JOURNALISM" TO "THE AGE OF PLENTY." THEN, FACED WITH A CHOICE ONLY BETWEEN "COMMUNIST COLLECTIVISM" OR "FASCIST CORPORATENESS" I WILL AT LAST FALL ON THE SIDE OF FASCISM.

W. T. SYMONS HERE... AND IF I MAY BE SO "BOLD" — IF YOU CHAPS WISH TO THROW THE GOOD MAJOR'S THEORIES "OUT THE POTHOUSE WINDOW", SO TO SPEAK, THEN BY ALL MEANS DO SO. HOWEVER, MANY STILL FEEL, AS I DO, THAT THE SOCIAL CREDIT MOVEMENT, SUCH AS IT IS, IS A "SPIRITUAL ASSOCIATION" OF A SOMEWHAT "GENTLE PERSUASION." DO HAVE SOME MORE REFRESHMENTS.

TOWARD YOU, DEAR SYMONS, I'M FEELING A "HEALTHY DISCONTENT..."

WANTED: LESS APPEAL TO THE MIDDLE CLASS + INTELLIGENSIA — AND MORE "LANGUAGE OF THE POTHOUSE"!

In 1925, Douglas and a few followers arranged the first national meeting of the various Social Credit study groups from around the country. The Swanick Conference, as it is now known, was the first and last time differing tendencies within Social Credit would ever meet in the same room. The movement quickly split into two recognizable camps: the centralists, who wanted to build a structured political party around Douglas' ideas; and the decentralists, who maintained, in the words of W.T. Symons, that "the movement as such is a spiritual association," and that it could be only pushed forward through the "gentle arts of persuasion."

The centralists withdrew from the conference and formed themselves into the Economic Freedom League; its founding members included Arthur Kitson, Frederick Soddy, an Oxford chemist and Nobel prize winner, and H.E.B. Ludlam, a Coventry printer. They were soon publishing their own journal, *The Age of Plenty*, with Ludlam as editor and "The Mighty Atom of Journalism" its slogan. The decentralists, claiming orthodoxy and allegiance to Douglas (although he refused office in this group, he was pleased to remain its *eminence grise*) remained a loosely articulated group of students and propagandists meeting together through dinner clubs and at an annual dinner.

The Economic Freedom League adopted an activist approach; its magazine promised "a healthy discontent that knows what it wants and is determined to get it"—a promise that would remained unfulfilled. Ludlam proved unable to hold the allegiance of his allies, one of whom described him as "a little man who wanted to be god." By 1930 he had alienated Kitson, who left to found the Monetary Reform League, and had begun a drift into fascism that would cut him off from most of his supporters. Ludlam distilled the ethical dilemma of the age into a simple choice between communism and fascist corporatism, and he chose the latter, making a direct appeal to the British Union of Fascists in the pages of *The Age of Plenty* (the fascists ignored him). By 1931 the Economic Freedom League had disappeared.

The failure of the Economic Freedom League seemed to justify the orthodox Douglasites in their quiet approach and their refusal to organize. Economic conditions in England seemed to be improving during the late '20s; there was no general perception of the coming crash and no public demand for monetary reforms. The public mood was optimistic: good times were felt to be just around the corner. Social Credit thinkers, of couse, did not share in the general optimism: a cardinal point of Douglas's theory held that the economy was poised on the brink of a catastrophe from which traditional financial techniques would be powerless to rescue it, and Douglas himself predicted in 1928 that the crash was only a year away.

ONE NIGHT AT THE MAJOR'S HOUSE...

This apocalyptic sense of the age caused anxiety among some of Douglas's followers, who felt that the small size of the movement made it vulnerable to annihilation by, for example, a general gas attack. This view, which appeared in a letter to *The New Age* was not shared by the majority, however, who seem to have awaited the coming crash with complacency—satisfied that the people of England, after suffering economic cataclysm, would naturally turn to Social Credit as the only logical answer.

But, while the orthodox Douglasites were calmly waiting for the apocalypse during the late '20s there was another force developing out on the fringes of British political life, within the ranks of an obscure back-to-the-woods movement named the Order of the Kibbo Kift and the...

The BIG SMOKE MIDDLE THING

The Kibbo Kift (from an old Cheshire phrase thought to mean "great strength") was a kind of Boy Scouts for grown-ups founded in 1920 by John Hargrave, an ex-Boy Scout leader who had become disaffected by the growing militarism and ultra-patriotism of the Scouting movement. He proclaimed the Kibbo Kift as "a body impulse to get Earth contact in a mechanical age," a slogan powerful enough to attract onto his advisory council the likes of Havelock

Ellis, Julian Huxley, Vilhjalmur Stefansson, Rabindranath Tagore and H.G. Wells, and to build among the Kin (as members of the Kift styled themselves) a small, loyal following.

JOHN HARGRAVE

JOHN HARGRAVE, a.k.a. White Fox, Wa-Whah-Goosh, headman of the Kibbo Kift, Leader of the Social Credit Party of Great Britain and Northern Ireland. Born in 1894 to a Quaker family, John Hargrave was an amateur of sociology and anthropology at an early age. At seventeen he was a cartoonist for the Evening Times and later worked in advertising. He had been a Boy Scout since age 14, and shortly before World War I became prominent in that "outlandish" new movement—to the extent that he became most likely to succeed Baden-Powell in its leadership. But even within the (at that time) unorthodox Boy Scout movement, Hargrave was himself unorthodox. His first book was *Lonecraft* (1913), written for Scouts who did not belong to any organized troop. (*Lonecraft* was dedicated to E.T. Seton, the popular Canadian writer of animal fiction and "Indian" stories.)

As a Quaker, Hargrave refused to bear arms in World War I: he served as a stretcher-bearer instead and was eventually wounded and invalided out in 1916. On his return to England he was dismayed to discover that the Scouting Movement had become a jingoist extension of the warmongering British establishment: no longer was it an alternative to industrialism, a counterculture of young people in opposition to the traditional values of imperialism.

From that time on, Hargrave's life can be seen as an attempt to recover a valid counterculture, and the Social Credit movement as the opportunity he took to attempt its achievement.

WA-WHAH-GOOSH, THE WHITE FOX, HERE, AND I FEEL IT APPROPRIATE TO OPEN MY SECTION WITH THE "KIBBO KIFT CAMPFIRE CEREMONY".

(I APPROACH THE FIRE IN A SCARLET ROBE PROFUSELY EMBELLISHED WITH GOLD FLAMES.)

" ENERGY, ENERGY, CEASELESS ENERGY
THE SILENT TERRIFIC ENERGY OF THE UNIVERSE.
THE FEARFUL AND WONDERFUL ENERGY OF THE ELECTRON. MICROCOSM AND MACROCOSM. ONE, ONE, ONE IS ONE.
FIRE, THE GREAT SYMBOL OF ENERGY— FIRE WHICH LEAPS BEFORE US, THE FIRE OF ALTHING—
O' MIGHTY FIRE OF LIFE! "

SOMEHOW LATER SOCIAL CREDIT HAS A PART IN ALL THIS...

58

The Kibbo Kift was conceived by Hargrave to be a movement of national and even world regeneration. He designed its ritual and special language along pseudo-Anglo-Saxon lines (the annual council was the Althing; the membership roll was the Kinlog; the branch office was the Thingcouncil; headquarters was the Big Smoke Middle Thing); and indicated his folk roots in a uniform of green and brown, with a Saxon cowl and jerkin, cloaked in the manner of the Prussian army. The philosophy of the Kibbo Kift was murky, combining obscure mysticism with a call for world unity, an end to unemployment and a new unspecified political order. The Kibbo Kift manifesto opens with the words, "All Life is Life. There is no Life but Life."

Reminding his followers (who numbered 236 in 1924) that "the proper function of the individual is to live splendidly," he saw in them an elite group whose destiny it was to act "as an instrument of social regeneration." But the Kin was not a political vanguard; it was hostile to organized political movements and considered them to be one of the many insidious "channels of mass-suggestion." Hargrave wanted to impose some kind of order on "the hot-headed, unsteady, easily-gulled Mass-mind," by introducing it to the "Positive Upright Fertilizing Principle."

Understandably, the numbers of this elite group remained small, and after a few years of rallying in the hills, making overnight hikes and issuing proclamations that usually concluded with the words "I have spoken," Hargrave began to feel that it was in danger of stagnating. In the late summer of 1924, he and a lieutenant went into the mountains of Wales, where they remained in seclusion for fourteen days. On their emergence, they carried with them the Dispensation of the New Law, a polemical treatise bidding the Kindred to read books on the New Economics, and in particular the works of Major C.H. Douglas.

Although Hargrave's personal conversion to Social Credit was abrupt (he must have first read Douglas in the pages of *Youth*, a university magazine edited by a friend who often featured essays by Douglas and his supporters), a year passed before he introduced Social Credit by name into the proceedings of the Kin: "We believe in Social Credit, the Just Price and the release of the individual from the position of machine minder!" It wasn't until 1927 that Social Credit theory officially became a part of the Kin's creed. Hargrave began writing enthusiastically about Social Credit in *The Nomad*—journal of the Kibbo Kift—while at the same time criticizing the movement: "The whole of the Social Credit movement is very weak in its psycho-sensory faculties."

Hargrave saw in the Social Credit movement an opportunity to revitalize the Kibbo Kift, and to save the world at the same time.

The Social Credit movement was by now split into the two camps represented by *The New Age* and *The Age of Plenty*. *The Age of Plenty* lacked the high tone of the older magazine, its contributors called themselves activists, and they directed much of their effort toward the unemployed. Hargrave was first drawn toward The Economic Freedom League for these reasons, and because he saw therein a chance to build the kind of paramilitary organization he had been dreaming about. He began to support the Economic Freedom League by organizing unemployed workers into (the happily named) Surplus Labour Groups, whose members swore an oath to uphold the demand for more purchasing power.

The Economic Freedom League took an immediate shine to Hargrave; he was a colourful and charismatic figure, coming in full uniform to their meetings, afraid neither to speak out nor to "get organized." *The Age of Plenty* quickly adopted the Kift: "this is a very healthy movement and any man worth his salt should be with it." In the opposing camp, *New Age* followers were equally attracted to him: he was seen a fresh alternative to the usual "speeches and discussions clogged like cold suet pudding." Hargrave displayed his power at his first League meeting, when he exhorted the delegates all to stand at his bidding, in a demonstration of the power of emotion over intellect.

"The Kin has something," wrote a *New Age* correspondent, "some throb of life—which the Social Credit movement needs: Faith in themselves." *The New Age* printed a favourable review of Hargrave's major work, *The Confession of the Kibbo Kift*, in which it was noted that the leader of the Kift had "drawn something useful from St. Paul, Mme. Blavatsky, Charlie Chaplin, Cromwell, Lao Tzu, Nietzsche, Noah and Tolstoy."

Representatives from both orthodox and activist Social Credit camps attended the Kift's Althing that spring, to take part in an elaborate, if somewhat bizarre, Fire Ceremony presided over by the charismatic Hargrave.

For some months Hargrave was able to use his sudden popularity to play off one Social Credit faction against the other. The Economic League made the strongest overtures toward the Kift, but they were collapsing under the unpopular Ludlam faster than they could regroup around Hargrave. One of the League members, George Hickling, broke away to organize unemployed workers in Coventry into Crusader Legions spearheaded by a new elite called the Iron Guard. Hickling's group flourished for a few months and seemed for a while to pose a threat to Hargrave's ascendancy. The Crusaders put forward a three-part slogan: demanding a national credit office, a price calculus, and the National Dividend. Douglas himself gave the Crusaders his blessing. But the mild-mannered Hickling was no match for Hargrave, who in a matter of weeks was able to sweep the Crusaders Legion and the Iron Guard into the Kift itself.

AS IT WENT...

1928 THE ECONOMIC PARTY
WELCOME TO ANOTHER SPLIT
IN THE SOCIAL CREDIT MOVEMENT
(No Refreshments Will Be Served)

AH! THE BLEEDER!

Coventry 1930

WELCOME TO THE COLLAPSE OF THE
ECONOMIC PARTY
(But do stay for the Establishment of
The Crusader Legion)

WELCOME TO THE IRON GUARD
The Inner Elite of
THE CRUSADER LEGION
(Bread and Water Served)

1930

WELCOME TO THE AMALGAMATION
of The Kibbo Kift, The Iron Guard
& The Crusader Legion
"NAME THE NEW MOVEMENT"
Big Draw at 9:00 pm

AND THE WINNER IS . . .

Almost overnight, Hargrave transformed the arcane Kibbo Kift into a modern political organization. The Thingcouncil became District Headquarters, and the Big Smoke Middle Thing, London Headquarters. The Saxonesque uniforms were replaced by the green shirts favoured by the Crusaders Legion; and the Kibbo Kift itself became the Green Shirt Movement for Social Credit. By 1933 all that remained of the old Kift was the mystical double-K symbol of the original Kindred; and even this had been reinterpreted: it was now said to represent the Double Key, with which the "Douglas door into the Promised Land" would be unlocked.

In one of his first Green Shirt speeches, Hargrave excitedly proclaimed the rapid approach of ...

An Economic Runymede ...

The Green Shirts seemed to prosper in the first years of the Depression. Major Douglas and his followers, dismayed to discover that the predicted Great Crash did not of itself bring the British people over to Social Credit, gingerly gave their blessing to Hargrave, and Douglas himself offered the Green Shirts the green Scottish tartan that he claimed for his family. The Green Shirts found a brief popularity among the general public: their colourful marches, strongly worded leaflets, country retreats and study groups for the out-of-work at least gave the unemployed something to do; and at the same time presented an alternative to the organized black-shirted Fascists led by Oswald Mosley.

For the Green Shirts, with all their paramilitary apparatus, were not Fascists; Hargrave explicitly denounced both fascism and communism, describing his position as "the third resolvent factor." And, whereas the Black Shirts espoused violence and the virulent anti-semitism that was sweeping most of the western world in the '30s, the Green Shirts, unlike Douglas, resisted racial theory and anti-semitism; their "unarmed military technique" found its most violent expression when a follower named Michael Murphy tossed a green brick through the window at 11 Downing Street (the home of the Minister of Finance). For this act, which found favour in the eyes of the public as well as the Green Shirts, Murphy was awarded the the coveted Green Oak Leaf, the Victoria Cross of the Green Shirt "army."

By 1933, any hope the Social Credit Movement felt seemed to centre in Hargraves and his organization. But the activist policies of the Green Shirts, while apparently boding well for Social Credit as a political movement, made the Major himself uneasy. In an attempt to maintain his central position in the movement, he announced the formation of the Social Credit Secretariat, a body that would extend recognition and legitimacy to Social Credit groups that kept within his own orthodoxy. As well, it would serve as a coordinating body for Social Credit groups that had begun to spring up in the Dominions.

For Social Credit ideas were beginning to find an enthusiastic audience in the colonies. Encouraged by this development, Douglas decided to embark on a world tour late in the winter of '33. The trip was a great success: his reception in Australia and New Zealand was overwhelming; and when he got to Western Canada he discovered a full-blown Social Credit political movement. Even the governments paid attention to him, inviting him to speak in national legislatures, and his trip was covered lavishly in the colonial newspapers.

Made confident by this new-found celebrity, he decided to take an active hand in the movement on his return to England by taking Social Credit into a national election—an unlikely move for a man who in the past had advised his followers to ignore the electoral process, and to "go to the polling booth and spoil your ballot by writing on it some such remark as 'a plague on all your houses'."

Douglas's electoral tactic was equally unlikely: he designed a campaign intended to coerce the traditional parties into adopting Social Credit, by asking voters to support only candidates (Tory, Liberal or Labour) who would pledge themselves to the National Dividend. Social Credit was not even to be mentioned by name; and the Secretariat put no candidates into the race.

Hargrave, unhappy with Douglas's quietist strategy, reacted by renaming his Green Shirt Movement the Social Credit Party of Great Britain and running a solitary candidate in Leeds.

The election of 1935 was a complete disaster for the Douglasites. Nowhere did the National Dividend pledges appear to influence the vote. Hargrave's candidate, however, pulled in a respectable 11% of the vote. Douglas responded by withdrawing his blessing from Hargrave, and revoking his green tartan. Hargrave reacted to Douglas's censure by disrupting the last large Social Credit meeting held in England, and declaring himself the only legitimate Social Credit leader in the world (the meeting was restored to order by the police).

Meanwhile, in Alberta, Canada, the first Social Credit government in the world was taking office, with the participation of neither Hargrave nor Douglas (each of whom, in his own way, would condemn the Albertans as incompetent dupes of the banking conspiracy.)

Over the next five years the British movement splintered again and again. *The New Age* expired, and was replaced by *Social Credit*; Orage reappeared for a time and published the *New English Weekly*. Maurice Reckitt, disillusioned with Douglas's leadership, tried to set up a new Secretariat on his own. From somewhere in the ranks emerged a new League to Abolish Poverty. Douglas founded another magazine, *The Social Crediter*, which was soon replaced by *Reality*; and later still by *The Fig Tree*.

Toward the end of the '30s, the Green Shirts ran afoul of the Public Order Act, which outlawed uniforms in political organizations; and by the onset of World War II had dwindled to almost nothing.

Social Credit never found a grass roots in England; spurned by a middle class preoccupied with the spectre of European fascism, it remained the plaything of eccentrics and tinkerers in the country of its birth. It found its strongest appeal among middle-class intellectuals alienated from their class but unwilling to align themselves with the proletariat. Some of these thinkers tried to involve themselves directly in the political life of the country—with what success we have seen—while others remained outside the political

BAH

"VEX NOT THOU THE BANKER'S MIND
(HIS WHAT?) WITH A SHOW OF SENSE,
VEX IT NOT, WILLIE, HIS MIND,
OR PIERCE ITS PRETENCE..."
— from "Alfred Venison's Poems: Social Credit Themes"
— by the POET OF TICHFIELD STREET
(who is really me — heh, heh)

"...ASSISTED
[TEN THOUSAND FATTED
BANKERS] BY 500
CURS." — AN IMPACT

"FRANCE IS LOSING ITS BREAD AND
WINE, ITS COFFEE WENT TO HELL
AFTER THE WAR." — S.C. — AN IMPACT

"THERE WILL
BE NO RED
REVOLUTION
IN ENGLAND"
— S.C. — AN IMP.

"I THINK MUSSOLINI'S
EFFICIENCY IS DUE TO THE MENTAL
QUALITY WHICH CAUSES HIM TO YELL
THAT THE "ECONOMIC MAN" IS ALL
BUNK... THAT NOBODY EVER SAW
"HOMINEM ECONOMICUM", AND THAT
WHEN YOU TALK TO 99 PERCENT OF
HUMANITY YOU'VE GOT TO USE JUST
ROUGH HORSE SENSE."
— from "SOCIAL CREDIT:
AN IMPACT — E. POUND

"THE GERMANS HAVE BEEN FED
ON ERSATZ, HAVING BEEN
BROKEN TO IT DURING THE WAR,
AND ARE THANKFUL FOR AN
OCCASIONAL LET UP."
— SOCIAL CREDIT — AN IMPACT

EZRA

"MARK FOUND NOTHING
TO CRITICIZE IN MONEY"
— "TELL THAT TO THE HALF-
MASTED SOCIALISTS. THEY
NEED IT. THEY NEED
TELLIN'; THEY NEED
AN AWFUL LOT OF
TELLING. THERE IS
NOTHING LESS CAP-
ABLE OF MENTAL MOTION
THAN A SOCIALIST, UNLESS
IT IS HIS SIDE-KICK,
THE BOLO."
— SOCIAL CREDIT: AN IMPACT

"SEE 'EM GO SLOUCHING THERE,
WITH COWED AND CROUCHING AIR
DUNDERING DULLARDS!
HOW THE WHOLE NATION SHOOK
WHILE MILORD BEAVERBROOK
FED 'EM WITH HOGWASH!"
— from "Alfred Venison's Poems" (heh, heh)

RECEIPT
ONE CAB FARE
TO
TICHFIELD
STREET

"THE POMPS OF BUTCHERY, FINANCIAL POWER
TOLD 'EM TO DIE IN WAR, AND THEN TO SAVE
THEN CUT THEIR SAVING TO THE HALF OR LOWER;
WHEN WILL THIS SYSTEM LIE DOWN IN ITS
GRAVE?"
— the Poet of
Tichfield Street

"SHYLOCKS
+ EUNICHS"...

arena, content to elaborate on the ethical and philosophical implications of Social Credit theory. Which brings us to a brief scrutiny of ...

Social Credit & the INTELLECTUAL ELITE

When A.R. Orage deserted *The New Age* three years after introducing Major Douglas to its readers, there remained with the journal another of his proteges, a self-described mystic named Dimitrije Mitrinovic. Mitrinovic's writings in *The New Age* were obscure at best, but after he lost Orage they became nearly opaque, and the new editor began to squeeze him out of the magazine. Miffed, Mitrinovic asked some friends to join him in a discussion group. After meeting in a number of different restaurants, the little vanguard settled on a place called the Chandos, and the Chandos Group was born.

The Chandos Group was a loose network of intellectuals of different backgrounds; they met fairly regularly for some years, to discuss problems of the day from a Social Credit perspective. Among its members were Maurice Reckitt and A.T.Symons, the ex-National Guildsmen already introduced in these pages; Hilderic Cousens, classical scholar and ex-secretary to Bertrand Russell; and various ex-Distributists, Anglican high and low churchmen, school teachers and socialist journalists. Somewhat on the fringe, but sharing the central interest in Social Credit were G.D.H. Cole, Lewis Mumford and American poets Ezra Pound and T.S. Eliot. (Eliot, whose poem *The Wasteland* is perhaps the most influential English poem of the century, never made the full commitment to Douglasism, claiming in the pages of *Social Credit* to "lack an economic mind.") The Chandos group managed to keep itself together for seven or eight years and published two books of general political observations reflecting its disdain for parliamentary democracy (which they described as "a quinquennial abdication of responsibility") and its uneasiness with the methods, if not the goals, of formal socialism.

EZRA POUND

Born 1895 in Hailey, Idaho; died 1972 in Rapallo, Italy. Ezra Pound left the USA in 1910 on a cattle ship, intending to devote his life to poetry and the arts. During his stay in England, he developed a reputation as a brilliant new poet and critic. He found a genial milieu in the pages of The New Age, where he first encountered the ideas of Major Douglas, whose ardent convert he remained for the rest of his life. Convinced that the path toward Social Credit lay in the new totalitarianism, he left England in the '20s to live in Mussolini's Fascist Italy, where he remained until his arrest by American troops in 1945. Charged with treason for his wartime propaganda activities but never tried, he was committed to a mental hospital instead, where he remained until 1958, when he was allowed to return to Italy. Rumours that Pound offered to move to Alberta when Social Credit achieved power there in 1935 (only to be refused by the Prophetic Bible Institute) cannot be confirmed. His famous long work, the Cantos, contains many arcane references to Social Credit theory and the economics of Major Douglas. Pound is considered to be one of the original modernists in English poetry, and his work has had an impact, directly or indirectly, on every poet writing in English since. In 1935 he published Social Credit: An Impact, dedicated to the Green Shirts of England. New Directions, the influential New York publishing house, was founded by James Loughlin in 1936 to publish Pound in America and to further the Social Credit cause. Pound was remembered by Gertrude Stein as the man with the beard who broke her chair and ate her tulips.

By the early '30s, when Orage returned to England to publish *The New English Weekly*, the Chandos Social Credit analysis was hardening along centralist totalitarian lines. The "new nationalism" that was infecting the European middle-classes began to percolate into the rarefied air of the Chandos Group and found its expression in Orage's new journal.

The Marquis of Tavistock, for instance, began contributing articles in favour of the corporate state; and Ezra Pound, one of Social Credit's loudest and most embarrassing adherents, began writing about the wonders of Fascism under Mussolini, comparing the Italian dictator favourably with Thomas Jefferson and Major Douglas. (Pound published *Social Credit: An Impact*, an incoherent polemic dedicated to the Green Shirts, and a book of doggerel Social Credit verse as well as numerous articles on Douglasism in little magazines.)

Other contributors took up the cause of Nazism, finding in it a "refreshing" attack on the system, a "resurgence of the soil against the asphalt, of the land against the big city." For a time there was even speculation that Hitler would come out for Social Credit: The Marquis of Tavistock claimed to have "personally interested Herr Hitler in our programme, although I am unable to say how far he or the Nazis are committed to it in Germany." Even after the war started in 1939, Social Credit sources would be claiming hopefully that Göring was still investigating the doctrine.

A strong anti-semitic bias began to inform the editorial pages of *The New English Weekly*. The editors, accused of racism by outraged readers, tried to defend themselves with the ingenuous observation that, although both Anglican and Catholic spokesmen had come out for Social Credit, no rabbi had yet embraced the Douglas system.

But organized fascism spurned flaky intellectuals bearing panaceas, even—perhaps especially—Social Credit ones. After all, the Douglas analysis was essentially a hedonistic one, with its notions of a Leisure Society and the freedom to be unemployed. Social Credit thinkers have always been attracted to "strong men" willing to take direct, if not necessarily democratic, action. But the true fascist, perceiving a kind of anarchy to lie at the heart of Social Credit, will in the final analysis, be repulsed by it.

The Social Credit flirtation with fascism was further compromised by the Spanish Civil War. Both *The New Age* (which was still publishing in 1933) and *The New English Weekly* supported the loyalist left against Franco, and opened their pages to leftist writers like George Orwell. (Mussolini and Hitler, of course, supplied arms and armies to Franco.) Social Credit found itself trying to support both ends against the middle: sympathetic to Italy and Germany on one hand, and loyalist Spain on the other. Unable to resolve this and other dilemmas within the framework of Douglasism, intellectuals began to abandon the Social Credit ship in growing numbers.

By the outbreak of World War II, what was left of the Social Credit intellectual tradition had distanced itself somewhat from European fascism. But the spectre of anti-semitism, always a temptation to the "conspiratorially-minded," would haunt its history into the '80s.

The Chandos Group was also a link between Social Credit commentators and the new school of Adlerian psychology known as Individual Psychology. Mitrinovic was first attracted to Adler's London discussion group in 1923; A.T. Symons and others soon followed him.

Adlerianism was similar to Social Credit in that it proposed a technical solution that could be applied immediately, without reference to past or future. Human impulses were to be accepted as basically sound; the problem was simply to establish whether or not they were properly organized. Symons suggested that both Douglas and Adler "took the world for a starting point," and for this reason were rejected by traditional socialists because they did not postulate a process reaching into the past and moving into the future, a process of conflict and periodic change: Adler and Douglas postulated a kind of instant evolution, with "no strife, no revenge."

Individual Psychology further offered, by analogy, a reason for the failure of mainstream economists and politicians to accept the Social Credit truths that could free the world: Adler had shown that patients could suffer terrible ill health even when there was nothing organically wrong with them—their sickness was the result of inaccurate perception. Symons used the Adlerian line to expand on Douglas' notion of the pyramid of power: "Douglas in the economic sphere has made precisely the same discovery that Adler has made in the psychological sphere ... that power over other men is the aim of the neurotic individual." Douglas acknowledged the connection too, noting his agreement "with the main thesis, that the craving for power is the focus of the world's ill-health."

The Chandos-Adler connection grew to include the Sociological Society, whose magazine was edited for some time by Lewis Mumford. The Sociological Society absorbed the Douglasites rapidly, and moved its offices to the headquarters of the Individual Pschycology movement, where a number of sub-groups achieved brief lives: The International Society of Individual Psychology; The Eleventh Hour Movement; The New Britain Group; and the New Europe Group. A stream of periodicals rose and fell: *New Britain* was eaten by *The Eleventh Hour Bulletin,* which in turn devoured *New Atlantis* (Mitrinovic's project) along with *New Albion* (A.R. Orage, editor), and *New Europe,* before reappearing as *New Britain* once again.

The dominant New Britain Group adapted the ideas of Rudolph Steiner's Anthroposophical Society to Social Credit and issued a cryptic motto: "Social Credit—National Guilds—The Threefold State: National, Imperial, European, and Planetary Federation in Devolution and Devolution in Federation." It was about this time that Adler withdrew from Social Credit and the successive incarnations of the Sociological Society, having perhaps decided that its compensations were not suited to his needs.

The New Britain movement achieved a higher level of success that any of the overt Social Credit movements, claiming a magazine circulation of 32ᶜooo copies a week in 1935. Harold MacMillan, the Red Tory, and Bertrand Russell were among its contributors, along with T.S. Eliot and J.T. Murphy, former shop steward and one-time communist. But the Chandos-Social Credit connection dried up with the departure of the Adlerians, and by the late '30s diehard Social Credit intellectuals had all withdrawn to the shell of *The New English Weekly.*

BEING AS HOW I AM BUT A SIMPLE [burd] OF PREY, AND A NATIONAL SYMBOL, SOCIAL CREDIT WAS NEVER MUCH TO MY, OR THE AMERICAN PEOPLE'S, "PROPENSITY", AND, WITH ALL DUE RESPECT TO JAMES LOUGHLIN IV. (QUITE THE OLD [burd] HIMSELF), THE ONLY SOCIAL PARTY "NOM DE GUERRE" OF ANY KIND I EVER HEARD OF FROM BOSTON WAS THE BOSTON SOCIAL "TEA" PARTY OF 1773.

ASK ANY OTHER "CONJUROR" OF THE "ETHERIAL SPHERES".

SOCIAL CREDIT In the USA

IN 1931, THE IRREPRESSIBLE A.R. ORAGE swept through New York City on a lecture tour. As a spokesman for the avant-garde, he drew large audiences of the curious and the thoughtful, and left behind him the barren seeds of an American Social Credit movement. Inspired by the example of The New Age, one Gorham B. Munson began publishing a journal of Social Credit opinion and the arts on behalf of the newly formed New Economics Group. Called The New Democracy, Gorham's journal featured the poetry of Ezra Pound in a column edited by young James Loughlin IV. Loughlin called his column New Directions; and in 1936, when he began publishing books, he kept the name for his publishing house. Still a Social Crediter in 1982, when he spoke in Vancouver, Canada (he claims to be the last survivor of the Boston Social Credit party), Loughlin is perhaps the most respected literary publisher in the U.S.

Social Credit failed to take root in American soil; a few senators and congressmen showed fleeting interest; poets William Carlos Williams and Archibald MacLeish toyed with it for a while; and a few tiny discussion groups coalesced in the eastern states and California. No coherent political movement ever emerged. Middle-class extremism in the U.S. would find its expression among the followers of populist governor Huey Long in Louisiana, and later in the broad support for Senator McCarthy in the paranoid witch hunts of the '50s.

The VISION

Alberta 1932–1971

COME TO AMERICA!!
Extravagant
Promises!

THE NORTHWEST FRONTIER

As recently as 100 years ago there were fewer than 1000 white people living on the part of the North American plain known today as Alberta. The Canadian government in Ottawa bought the territory in 1869 from the Hudson's Bay Company (which had been granted it by the King of England), and over the next thirty years displaced the native Cree, Sarcee, Stoney, and Blackfoot peoples onto reservations to make way for one of the largest European immigrations in history.

Peasants and poor farmers in England, Germany, Scandanavia and the Ukraine were enticed to leave the old world by extravagant promises of a better life in the new. These Europeans were joined by Finns and Belgians from the US states of Michigan and Minnesota, and later by Mormons from Utah.

By 1891 there were 17,500 white people in Alberta, and by 1911, when the big rush ended, the population was 374,000.

These homesteading immigrants were expected to develop a farming economy that could supply the rest of the rapidly industrializing Empire with wheat and beef. Financial and political power over the western provinces of Canada lay in the eastern metropolis, in the big banks and the Dominion government, which represented the British Empire in North America.

Alberta (named after one of Queen Victoria's daughters) was declared a Canadian province in 1905, with its legislature in Edmonton. Bordered on the west by the Rocky Mountains, on the south by the US state of Montana, on the north by the 60th parallel and on the east by a line drawn along the 110th degree of longitude, it encompasses 661,000 square kilometres of tundra, prairie and foothills.

OH, GIVE ME A HOME...

A PROPHET Is BORN

Major Douglas had expected the Crash of 1929 to bring the British people to their senses, and cause them naturally to turn to Social Credit for relief; in this he had been sadly mistaken. But the ensuing Great Depression of the '30s affected most of the world; and few British subjects felt its effects as profoundly as farming families on the Canadian prairies—thousands of whom were plunged into abject poverty within a few short years.

Unknown to the Major, the Social Credit cause would take root in those dry prairies and find its unlikely prophet in a fundamentalist Baptist preacher and high school principal named William Aberhart, a man destined to become the leading political figure in Social Credit history.

For the Canadian province of Alberta, the '30s was a time of economic desperation: as world grain and beef prices plummeted, average yearly farm incomes dropped from a high of about $2000 in 1927 to an almost unbelievable low of $54 in 1933. Thousands of families were thrown onto the dole; some years there was no point in even trying to market crops—they were burned as fuel instead. During the first four years of the '30s, 14,000 motor vehicles simply disappeared from Alberta roads and half the registered telephones went out of service. The flour sack became an important household textile. As the farmers lost their livelihoods, small businesses lost their customers, and the malaise deepened.

Alberta's economy in the early '30s provides a classic example of the helplessness of the small producer in a world of centralized credit and distant markets. Farmers were almost without exception at the mercy of banks thousands of miles away in the industrial and financial centre of Canada. They paid high interest rates on their mortgages when they had any money, and lost their farms and livelihoods when they didn't. With no control over the world grain market, they were forced to accept prices unrelated to their costs.

In the first third of the century, Canada was dominated politically by the Liberal and the Conservative parties: roughly equivalent to the Whigs and Tories of England. These parties represented factions of the eastern Canadian money and business interests who controlled the flow of money and credit to and from the western provinces. Eastern manufacturers were further protected by a system of tariffs that made it impossible for secondary industry to develop in the West.

By 1932 the exploitative nature of east to west in Canada had made itself abundantly clear to many who lived on the Prairies: the farmers were the colonists of the 20th century. They worked their land in the interests of profit-making "middle" capitalists in the east, who in their turn represented foreign capitalists in England.

In the early '30s, all credit in Canada was tightly controlled by a centralized oligarchy of large eastern banks.

In 1921, the United Farmers of Alberta (UFA), a populist movement that initiated cooperatively-run grain elevators, took political power away from the Liberal Party in Alberta, to form provincially the first agrarian government in the country.

The UFA fought to weaken eastern control over the Alberta economy, and to some extent succeeded, although they could never affect the world wheat price or the big banks' stranglehold on credit.

By the mid-30s, government and private debt in Alberta had reached three-quarters of a billion dollars, and there was almost no income, private or public, to offset it.

The provincial economy was bottoming out: by 1933 farm incomes had fallen to 6%, and world grain prices to 10%, of their pre-depression levels; small business income was down by 36%. In the east, things weren't much better: industrial wages and salaries had fallen by a third and stock dividends were down 40%. Only one sector of the national economy was showing growth: income from bond interest and mortgages was up 13%.

School boards in Alberta found themselves with no money to pay teachers. In many rural schools, the annual budget covered one box of chalk and one package of foolscap paper. Teachers were paid in produce when they were paid at all.

In the cities, farmers and unemployed workers demonstrated in the streets. Young men rode the rails from coast to coast. At an Edmonton hunger march in 1932, police beat down demonstrators singing *The Red Flag* and *The Internationale*, songs of the Communist party.

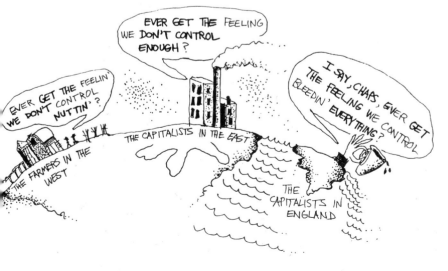

By 1934, the UFA government in Alberta had run out of answers. Unable to help the people of Alberta, it allied itself with the Ottawa government to put down protest and dissidence by any means possible. All levels of government were helpless in the face of general economic failure. Not surprisingly, many Albertans began to look to the church for guidance during these hard times, and in particular to a man of the church who claimed to have heard their lamentation, and was prepared to lead them out of the wilderness.

WILLIAM ABERHART

BIBLE BILL ABERHART was born in 1879 on a dairy farm in southern Ontario. His father was a German immigrant, his mother British. He was "a big strong boy who worked hard," and loved to go to Evangelical revival meetings. As a teenager, he used to imitate the old time preachers out in the backyard, haranguing the barnyard creatures from behind a pine stump.

He finished his education and became a school teacher, moving out west to Calgary in 1910. In 1915 he became principal of Crescent Heights High School.

Aberhart's special talent was organization; he ran his school like a well-oiled machine: tasks neatly assigned; written procedures for nearly every eventuality. His office was crammed with diagrams, flowcharts and organizational tables. He was a firm believer in rote learning and logical organization of subject matter.

A big man, six feet tall and weighing nearly 260 pounds, he liked to say that he weighed an eighth of a ton. He was a born showman and fostered good publicity for his school. His teachers generally liked him, and they could count on his support in confrontations with parents. Although he opposed evolutionary theory, he did nothing to stop its being taught in the school.

Many people were in awe of him. He was a hard-working, dynamic administrator, rising at 6:00 am, working all day and through the lunch hour (he always took a bag lunch). Evenings he worked at the Prophetic Bible Institute until the early hours of the morning.

...APART FROM PRACTICING MY EARLY PREACHING BY BEATING MY FIST ON A PINE STUMP IN THE BACKYARD AND YELLING AT THE BARNYARD CREATURES, I ALSO LIKED TO SAY LATER I WEIGHED AN EIGHTH OF A TON, AND LATER, I LIKED TO SAY: "THE FLOW OF CREDIT IS THE BLOODSTREAM OF THE STATE"; AND LATER THAN THAT, I LIKED TO SAY: "YOU CANNOT GET TO HEAVEN WITH A BIBLE IN ONE HAND AND A FORECLOSURE MORTGAGE OF YOUR NEIGHBOR'S HOUSE IN THE OTHER!" HOW'S THAT FOR APPLES?

AND THERE'S NO SMOKING IN SCHOOL EITHER!

260 lbs.

THUMP!

PORTRAIT OF ABERHART BY NICHOLAS DE GRANDMAISON, BANFF - ALTA.

...IN EDMONTON LEGISLATIVE BUILDING.

In the first years of the Depression, William Aberhart's life was entirely bound up in religion and education. He revealed to his friends and colleagues no real interest in public affairs, and his concern with contemporary events was almost wholly a function of his understanding of the prophecies of Daniel. His sense of the future course of humankind derived from his study of the Book of Revelations (which had once led him to to conclude that the world was going to end in 1934), and it is likely that he saw the first years of the Depression as heralding the biblical Apocalypse.

Aberhart ran his highschool like a drillmaster. One of his teachers has said of him: "He was a good dog trainer. He insisted on mechanical memory, without thought or reasoning behind it. 'Never mind why,' he would say to his students." An ex-student reports: "He was a born organizer, and he applied his great ability to the organization of the rules of arithmetic. We were all in awe of the old man, and so we always did *his* homework."

"He seemed to have a mind like a cabinet," says another of his teachers, "full of little drawers opening and closing. He had a perfectly marvellous mechanical memory; he could go into a room and teach a class only once, and the next time he could call every student by name. He could remember anything, but he couldn't *think* about it or *analyze* it. He accepted ideas completely—so it's not surprising that he became a hopeless fundamentalist and a Social Crediter."

But Aberhart drew people to him through personal magnetism. A teaching colleague remembers him as "one of the unforgettable persons I have known. He was a great noise and a great light. In his presence one felt as if one were in a magnesium flare."

Aberhart was a Christian fundamentalist who rejected the idea that scripture should be re-interpreted in light of new knowledge. His intellectual life was devoted to the ideas of scriptural authority and individual conscience, a struggle that he took into the modern Presbyterian and Methodist Churches in Calgary. His ability to argue doctrine and dogma earned him enemies in the middle-of-the road Protestant churches, and finally friends in the Westbourne Baptist Church.

He maintained that the Bible was an unerring and infallible authority. An anti-modernist, he accused scholars who sought to re-translate the Bible of "rushing in where angels fear to tread." Bible study was his first love. He committed long passages of scripture to memory, and rarely hesitated to quote from them whenever the occasion seemed to call for it. At Westbourne Baptist he began a series of highly popular Bible classes and attracted hundreds of people into the congregation.

By 1932, William Aberhart was well-known to a wide-spread prairie community of farmers, shopkeepers and other small entrepreneurs. He was a fiery evangelical orator who discovered a natural vehicle for his religious message in the new-fangled medium of radio. His first broadcasts in 1925 were mild performances, but once he gained a radio voice, he found an eager constituency in the huge audience that tuned in to hear him Sunday evenings: a congregation that soon exceeded 350,000. His Back to the Bible Hour drew more listeners in than the Jack Benny Show.

The congregation of Westbourne Baptist grew rapidly with the increasing popularity of its unofficial preacher. By the end of 1926 its night classes were packed, and a large correspondence course was underway. The need for a full-time school was clear. With his proposal to found a Prophetic Bible Institute, William Aberhart was unknowingly laying the foundation for a powerful political machine. Throughout 1927 he exorted his radio parishioners to donate money to the new project.

Aberhart organized the fund-raising for the Institute himself, plugging the project every Sunday on the radio. He sold "sods" for a hundred dollars each, and bricks for five dollars. In October

1927, just about a year after he conceived the idea, the Prophetic Bible Institute opened its doors.

Calgary 1927
WELCOME TO THE
Prophetic Bible Institute
("Out where the handclasp's a little stronger")

"Everlasting happiness of the righteous and the awful and everlasting misery of the unbelieving wicked, in a literal lake of fire, prepared for a real, personal devil and his angels"

Uplift the Spirit
Biblical Proofs & Systematic Theology
Sacred History & Bible Geography
Evangelism & Public Speaking
Sunday School Teaching, Sewing, Music,
Typewriting, Millinery, Domestic
Science & Motor Mechanics

FURSHLI

... I GOTTA LEARN ALL THAT?

Doctrinal Notes
Infallibility of the Bible
Immaculate Conception
Divine Creation
Physical Resurrection of the Dead

The Institute recruited students from the farms of the prairies, British Columbia, the northern USA and Alaska. Students were expected to lead lives of "separation from all harmful and spritually degrading pursuits"; their tuition was free. The staff—all volunteers—were hand-picked by Aberhart from among people who had taken his Bible study courses at Westbourne.

The Prophetic Bible Institute prospered in the latter years of the '20s, and right through the Wall Street Crash of 1929. Aberhart kept his position as high school principal by day, and carried out his evangelical work at night and on weekends.

Aberhart's Christianity was a personal, not a social faith: the salvation of the individual was its only concern. In its first years the Bible Institute, like its founder, ignored the problems of secular society in the conviction that personal communion with the Saviour was the highest goal toward which humanity could strive.

But as the Depression deepened, both the Institute and Crescent Heights High School began to feel its ominous effects. Students in both institutions began to wear patched clothing, and it was clear to the teachers that many of them were not eating properly. Children were fainting in class. And as donations dwindled, it became increasingly difficult to finance the Institute and the radio series.

In 1931, civic and provincial authorities, seeing no way to deal with the terrible effects of an economy in violent recession, and looking for a scapegoat, launched an attack on the education system. Suddenly the schools were too expensive; tax dollars were being "wasted" on teachers who were characterized as barely competent to teach. Teachers and parents who opposed the move to cut back education went unheard: the major Edmonton and Calgary papers and the chairman of the Calgary school board supported the attack loudly. (The Board chairman went on record as seeing education cutbacks as a way to "put the fear of God into those Reds.")

Alberta teachers took a 30% cut in pay in the spring of 1932. Aberhart avoided public comment, but privately he was feeling pressure to take some kind of action. That spring, graduates from his high school went directly onto the relief lines, and many of his old students were losing their jobs—some of whom turned to him for help. All he could offer them was prayer, although when pressed by a student to "do something about the economic situation," he was heard to say, enigmatically: "The Gates of Hell shall not prevail against it."

As a community leader, Aberhart naturally felt obliged to take note of worsening conditions in Alberta. But not being a secular man, he could find no secular solutions.

He suffered a direct blow at the end of the 1932 school year, when a favorite Grade 12 student, unable any longer to bear his family's wretched circumstances, took his own life.

Filled with foreboding, Aberhart went to Edmonton a few days after the funeral, to mark matriculation exams. There he fell in with a colleague named Charles M. Scarborough, who for some years had been trying to interest Aberhart in the ideas of a certain Major Douglas—a British mechanical engineer who had developed a theory of economic reform he called Social Credit. Scarborough was a devout student of the Major's and had formed a Social Credit study group in Edmonton.

Aberhart had never shown any interest in Scarborough's political ideas and had always resisted his overtures. But this time, he was in the mood to talk about politics and economics; he found the discussion compelling enough to stay up all night reading a Social Credit primer that Scarborough left with him. (The book was *Unemployment or War* by Maurice Colbourne, a popularizer of the Douglas system.)

As the early summer sun rose that June morning in 1932, William Aberhart put down the book. At 56 years of age, he had received his revelation.

And Charles M. Scarborough had unleashed a whirlwind.

The ALBERTA GOSPEL

That fateful summer William Aberhart immersed himself in Social Credit. He read all of the published work of Major Douglas (memorizing much of it) and any of the commentaries he could get his hands on. He became a man possessed by a vision. The September meeting of the Bible Institute's Board of Management convened at the Tea Kettle Inn in Calgary; and there he first proposed to introduce Social Credit doctrine into his Sunday broadcasts:

> "My friends, I ask you: what is the root of all the poverty around us, while we live in the midst of potential plenty? Is it God's will that we suffer this way? We need men of good will to lead us out of this desert!"

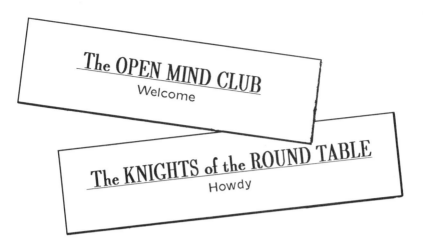

The OPEN MIND CLUB
Welcome

The KNIGHTS of the ROUND TABLE
Howdy

The Back to the Bible Hour became a sounding board for Social Credit. By the end of 1932, the Prophetic Bible Institute was offering a series of lectures devoted to the Douglas system, and the daily mail contained hundreds of requests for more information from his huge radio congregation. The first study groups Aberhart led himself, using his teaching methods to drill into new recruits the essentials of Douglas's theory. The publishing arm of the Institute began to distribute his lectures in pamphlet form throughout the province.

Compelled by his vision to go outside the church, Aberhart began to address the secular world as well. He spoke for the first time to a non-religious public meeting at the Canadian Legion Memorial Hall in Calgary, where he unveiled in more detail the Social Credit idea of monetary reform, and the need to get purchasing power into the hands of the general population, in order to defeat the worsening economic situation. It wasn't long before Social Credit was a catchword in secular circles too, and a popular topic in discussion groups such as the Knights of the Round Table and the Open Mind Club.

The first publications issued by the Bible Institute were known as the White Leaflets; each contained a short exposition by Aberhart, followed by questions for the student, and a brief summary of a chapter of Douglas's *Social Credit*.

In the spring of 1933, the Coloured Leaflets appeared. These were brief schematic summaries of Douglas' *Credit Power and Democracy* and were used to train speakers at the Institute. Popular demand for the Coloured Leaflets was so great over the next two years that many reprintings would be required.

About the time of the first Bible Institute lectures on Social Credit, Aberhart organized a private Social Credit study group of thirty close supporters. He led them carefully through the details of the theory, and drilled them relentlessly in its workings. In this original Group of Thirty he would later find his apostles: people willing and properly schooled to carry the Social Credit creed to the people.

For the first year of his involvement with Social Credit, Aberhart sought to encourage the public and its leaders to embrace monetary reform along Douglas lines. His campaign was an educational one; like Douglas in England, he felt that reform could be enacted by any elected government. But unlike Douglas, Aberhart's personal life had always been devoted to the salvation of mankind, and as he saw in Social Credit an earthly extension of that salvation, he worked more and more fervently for the cause. The effect on his followers was electric. Social Credit swept the province in a tidal wave of popular enthusiasm, and became a major force even before journalists on the big newspapers or the politicians in the main line parties began to notice.

Aberhart and his young assistant Ernest Manning toured the province in the spring and summer of 1933. Five days a week, twice a day, they lectured in community halls, churches, farmers' backyards, general stores and on small town main streets, carrying the doctrine to the people. (Weekends they were back in Calgary for the Sunday broadcast.) Their dedication and energy were manifest. And everywhere they went, they were met by the people who had been listening to Aberhart on the radio since 1925.

ERNEST MANNING

ERNEST MANNING was 19 years old when he answered the call of the newly formed Calgary Bible Institute. Before that, after leaving school in grade eight, he had worked on his parents' farm in the rural community of Rosetown, Saskatchewan. He was a tinkerer, and had an old Model T Ford which he stripped down and named "the Bazoo." In 1924, when he was 16, he bought a mail-order radio kit with a 100-foot antenna, and the Manning family, like so many farming people, joined the Radio Age. Within a year they were part of William Aberhart's far-flung congregation of the air.

Ernest was a shy boy, poker-faced and sedate. He had never been away from the farm when he heard Aberhart summon young people to Calgary to learn about Christ. When the Institute opened that fall, Ernest Manning was the first student to enroll. He came to Aberhart's notice the next year, and a strong friendship developed between them. By 1930, Manning was secretary of the Institute, living and working in Aberhart's house. He became part of the Back to the Bible Hour, and developed a radio voice so much like Aberhart's that few people could tell them apart.

Manning's destiny was interwoven from the beginning with Aberhart's; until the older man's death they were rarely apart. He followed him in the church and in the party, and would eventually take up the stewardship of both the Social Credit movement and the Prophetic Bible Institute.

...ALTHOUGH SEDATE AND POKER-FACED, I WAS THE FIRST STUDENT TO ENROLL IN BILL'S **CALGARY BIBLE INSTITUTE** AND A STRONG FRIENDSHIP HENCEFORTH DEVELOPED BETWEEN US— BUT GET A LOAD OF SEDATE ME IN THE '50's WHEN I BECOME PREMIER FOR AWHILE (HEH, HEH)... I WILL ALWAYS MISS "the BAZOO" THOUGH, BUT AS BILL SAYS: "*WHAT CAN THE RIGHTEOUS DO?*"

COME IN BAZOO — COME IN!

Throughout rural Alberta, farmers, shopkeepers and their families were all eager to hear the details of a plan that promised to do away forever with ...

Poverty in the Midst of Plenty

Aberhart based his Social Credit ideas on Douglas's National Dividend and the Just Price. But whereas the Major had spent years designing the complex mechanisms needed to measure the Real Credit of the nation, and to set and maintain a Just Price, Aberhart was boldly proposing rough-and-ready direct applications after only a few months of study.

Douglas's National Dividend he translated into a Basic Dividend, which he proposed to set at $25.00 per month, in credit, to be issued to every citizen in the province:

> This is to guarantee everyone the bare necessities of life without basing it on work. Salaries, wages, commissions, etc, are to be in addition to the Basic Dividend.

Twenty-five dollars was a considerable sum in the early '30s, and appears to have been an arbitrary figure set by Aberhart more as an example than a calculated amount. But the exemplary $25.00 payment caught the imagination of the people so forcefully that it became Social Credit policy before it could be justified mathematically (and before there was even a Social Credit Party, for that matter). Aberhart would have to develop some pretty strong arithmetic in order to calculate a Real Credit for the province able to sustain such big payments.

Aberhart's Just Price was equally straightforward:

> Prices would be controlled automatically by the application of the following formula:
>
> Market Price=Consumption/Production X Total Cost
>
> So that: If 50000 pairs of shoes costing $6 each should be produced, and only 40000 sold to Consumers, the price would automatically be reduced to 4/5 of $6.00=$4.80 per pair, in order to increase Consumption to the level of Production.
>
> Only when production equals consumption is the total cost of the goods produced covered by their sale. In other words, the principle of profit is abolished.
>
> Automatic Price Control will apply to the price of all necessities: food, clothing and shelter.

Social Credit appealed first to Aberhart because it was a mathematical solution to economic problems: it could be expressed in formulas, equations and diagrams. Furthermore, it was altruistic;

its ideology could be expressed in terms of efficiency: it promised to deliver the greatest good to the greatest number by the most efficient means.

In a very real sense, Aberhart's Social Credit vision was apocalyptic: it promised to usher in a new age by the mere application of simple arithmetic. It was as if a kind of secular Second Coming were at hand.

Most importantly, Aberhart's Social Credit required Faith: Faith in the basic theory, Belief in Real Credit. If the people believed in it, it had to work.

As a technical theory, Social Credit could be expressed in convincing metaphors. In his Yellow Pamphlet (which purists in the movement would attack for its "crudity"), Aberhart described the flow of credit as the bloodstream of the state:

The bloodstream metaphor was compelling, and Aberhart made good use of it in his speeches and pamphlets. He identified the

Financial Interests, a kind of evil tourniquet cutting off the source of life, simply as "The Fifty Bigshots," much to the delight of the crowd. The Bigshots, it followed, were responsible for "so much poverty in the midst of so much plenty"—a phrase that quickly became a slogan.

Aberhart's rhetoric was always colourful and convincing. He never dwelt on the technical details of managing a Social Credit epoch, but claimed instead that specialists would look after those things: all the people had to do was get the politicians to bring in those experts. Social Credit was like electricity, he was fond of saying: you don't have to understand it; all you have to do is push the button and you get light.

In less that a year, Social Credit became a household word in Alberta, among a rural people happily ignorant of its roots in the English avant garde and the underconsumptionist tradition. At the same time the established political parties, along with business leaders and journalists, ignored Aberhart's new economic dogma completely. In fact, Social Credit might have swept the hinterland unopposed, but for the perennial ...

Questions of Orthodoxy & the Correct Line

For some years, Social Credit had been known within certain circles of quiet Canadians, who, like Charles M. Scarborough, had become familiar with Douglasism through connections in the U.K. As Aberhart and Manning were sweeping the backwoods of Alberta with the Social Credit message in the summer of 1933, some of these more orthodox thinkers, dismayed to hear their doctrine in the mouths of fundamentalist upstarts, banded together into a New Age Club under the leadership of a college-trained businessman named Charles G. Palmer. They quickly affiliated with the London Secretariat, and began a parallel "educational" campaign aimed at discrediting Aberhart and putting "correct" Social Credit ideas before the public.

In the long run, the participation of the New Age group, along with other orthodox groups like the Open Mind Club and the Toronto-based Douglas Credit League, helped Aberhart's cause by interesting elements of the urban middle class in Social Credit. But for a brief period of about ten weeks in 1934, just as the movement was becoming a public issue, they seemed likely to succeed in their efforts to displace Aberhart as acknowledged leader of the movement.

The orthodox Social Creditors focussed their argument on the BNA Act, the document that served as a constitution for the colonial Dominion of Canada. Under its terms, they argued, the provinces did not have sufficient authority to introduce monetary reform; therefore the movement had to develop a federal, not a provincial, mandate directed toward the central government in Ottawa. They attacked details of Aberhart's version of Social Credit as well, as he had expressed it in his Yellow Pamphlet, *The Douglas System of Economics.* Aberhart stood up well under the increasingly public criticism of the orthodox, but he weakened when the London Secretariat, having been alerted to the contents of the pamphlet by the Calgary New Age Club, repudiated it in a letter sent to both Aberhart and the New Agers (who gleefully made it public.)

105

Aberhart startled his followers by impulsively announcing in the Calgary papers that he was preparing to give "his last address on the Douglas system" at the Bible Institute. On the evening appointed, February 27, 1934, a huge crowd turned out to learn what he meant. It was a memorable night: many in the audience wept openly as the man they considered to be a prophet described the persecution he was suffering at the hands of the "Toronto faction." He reaffirmed his faith in a vision of a Social Credit Alberta, and at the climax of the meeting, announced his resignation as President of the Central Council Social Credit League (as the secular arm of the Bible Institute had come to be known).

The crowd went wild. An impassioned disciple leapt onto the platform to deliver a speech (described by an onlooker as "incoherent and frenzied") in defense of Aberhart, and to make a resolution protesting the accusations of the Open Mind Club. The resolution passed unanimously.

Aberhart, on the verge of tears, yielded to the will of the crowd. He offered to make his resignation temporary by stepping aside from active leadership until Major Douglas himself could come to Alberta and straighten everything out. It was a dramatic move, injecting almost unbearable suspense into the struggle between factions. For the Major was then on his tour of the Commonwealth, and that very night was slowly making his way toward the western shore of Canada. . .

A Prairie Sojourn:
The Major In Alberta

Aberhart and Manning had done their work well among the rural communities of Alberta, where the governing United Farmers Association drew its greatest support: by early 1934, the UFA grassroots was shot through with Social Credit advocacy. Pressure from the ranks of the UFA had forced the government to take notice of Social Credit, and in February of that year to invite Major Douglas himself to Alberta as "reconstruction advisor."

Social Credit in Alberta was still in its pre-political stage: its factions, while fighting among themselves for primacy, shared the opinion that any political party could implement the doctrine as well as another. The UFA's invitation to Douglas was designed to appease discontented voters and to de-fuse a growing political threat, as much as it was a serious attempt to comprehend a new monetary system. Aberhart himself, although he now held no official position in the movement, spoke before a government committee struck to investigate Social Credit in March, along with New Agers and Open Minders who endeavoured further to discredit him, while espousing orthodox doctrine.

The Open Mind Club saw in Douglas's visit the opportunity to finally discredit Aberhart, and with this end in mind, organized a public meeting with Douglas as guest speaker and the Calgary Canadian Club as co-sponsor. William Aberhart was carefully excluded from the list of platform guests, but when the announcement went out to the press, the Open Minders were deluged by protests from the Calgary rank and file, and, two days before the meeting, were forced to invite him to sit (but not to speak) on the guest platform.

Aberhart, in an unofficial capacity, continued his Sunday broadcasts, developing a Social Credit agenda on the air while Central Council administration was carried out by his orthodox opponents. When Douglas got off the boat in Vancouver, Aberhart called to invite him on the air. Douglas refused, saying that he had already accepted the Open Minders' invitation to speak in public. And when the Major arrived in Edmonton, he elbowed Aberhart aside on the train platform, and went off with the official leaders.

Aberhart was tempted to refuse his own belated invitation to the public meeting, but his followers would not agree: railway workers in the Ogden Shop threatened to break up the meeting if he didn't go. Not wanting his cause to suffer violent demonstration, Aberhart at last relented, and showed up at the Calgary Armouries on the night of April 8, 1934.

April 8, 1934— Calgary Armouries Welcomes you to the First High-Profile Event in Canadian Social Credit History
Nervous Energy will be Evident
...A SIMPLE BLEEDING ENOUGH REQUEST, I DARE SAY. (I ONLY LEARNED LATER THAT IT WAS ALL AN ATTEMPT TO DISCREDIT MR. ABERHART, THE QUESTIONABLE ROGUE WHO'D BEEN MESSING ABOUT WITH MY ORIGINAL SOCIAL CREDIT THEORIES)...
...ORIGINALLY, THIS BLOKE WASN'T TO ATTEND THE SHOW, BUT DUE TO SOME STINK PUT UP BY THE LOCAL RABBLE, HE WAS FINALLY INVITED TO ATTEND AS A SORT OF "SUNDRY" GUEST OF HONOR...
...IT WAS AS I WAS INTO THE SECOND HOUR OF MY LECTURE THAT I BEGAN TO SENSE A "NERVOUS ENERGY" BUILDING IN THE BLEACHER SEATS (RELIGIOUS ZEALOTS AND RUFFIANS FOR ABERHART I SUSPECTED) WHICH SUDDENLY CULMINATED IN A "FOOTBALL-LIKE RUSH" TO THE PLATFORM...
GRRRRR-
SLURP!
...IT WAS AT THIS POINT I DEEMED IT PRUDENT TO RETIRE WITH SPEED, BUT NOT BEFORE CHALLENGING MR. ABERHART TO THE QUEEN'S RULES IN FIVE MINUTES IN THE CLOAKROOM...

The Armouries meeting was the first high-profile public event in the Canadian chapter of Social Credit history: its chairman was a city alderman and president of the Canadian Club who said in his introductory remarks that, if Major Douglas had a plan "to bring a feeling of order and security out of the chaos," he would be "the greatest human benefactor this country and this world has ever seen"; the Mayor of Calgary made an equally enthusiastic welcoming speech.

But the crowd was there for Aberhart. When he mounted the platform to take his seat cries of "We want Aberhart!" erupted throughout the hall. The band vainly struck up a raucous tune to drown them out. Even the Mayor was interrupted by shouted demands for Bible Bill; to calm the audience, he had to hint that Aberhart might speak after Douglas.

Douglas himself spoke for two hours in an unperturbed monotone, lecturing the audience on Social Credit fundamentals with which most of them were already familiar, while remaining elusive on the subject of a Social Credit plan for Alberta. As he droned on, the audience grew increasingly restive, and frequently interrupted him with cries for Aberhart. Douglas managed finally to conclude without having once mentioned Aberhart's name. An angry murmur spread through the hall as the vote of thanks was offered, and then a contingent from the bleachers rushed onto the floor and stormed the platform, crying "Aberhart, Aberhart!" The chairman frantically cut off the speaker and signalled for the band strike up God Save the King. But the uproar is reported to have been so great that no one could hear the music, and the King of England went, however briefly, unreverenced by his subjects in the Calgary Amouries.

Somehow the platform guests made their way out of the hall and into the cloakroom, where Aberhart and Douglas confronted each other in an encounter soon to become legend in Social Credit circles. Aberhart apparently opened the exchange by accusing Douglas of trying to sabotage his efforts and the Alberta Social Credit movement in general. Douglas responded by suggesting that Aberhart's grasp of Social Credit theory was tenuous, and that the Yellow Pamphlet should be pulped. A small crowd gathered as a vicious quarrel developed between the two men, who began to abuse each other harshly with what is reported to have been "rough language." Unhappily for the student of history, the witnesses were unwilling to repeat what they had heard; one of them, who would say no more, spoke for all when she said, "It was really awful, just a terrible thing."

The Armouries meeting, and Douglas's testimony before the government investigating committee, served to keep Social Credit on front pages throughout the province for most of April 1934. Douglas successfully avoided further contact with Aberhart and finally returned to England with his wife. (Mrs. Douglas had formed a slightly more sympathetic notion of Aberhart, his followers having arranged a "coincidental" meeting at a tea party held in her honour.) The Social Credit rank and file were glad to see Douglas go; he was perceived generally to be a cold fish, inimical if not dangerous to the Alberta movement.

The Armouries meeting, and the cloakroom encounter, only strengthened Aberhart's position. The New Agers had installed their own president, Gilbert McGregor, in Aberhart's place; but after the Douglas visit, majority sentiment in the Social Credit League hardened behind Aberhart, and the hapless Gilbert became a pariah in their eyes. He resigned in May and Aberhart was thrust back into his old position by popular acclaim.

While a UFA government committee continued to ponder the implications of Social Credit theory, Aberhart moved quickly to assure himself undisputed control of the movement. He swept the New Agers and the Open Minders out of the executive, and within a few weeks, out of the movement all together. He installed Ernest Manning as secretary and Mrs. F.G. Grevett as vice-president. (Mrs. Grevett was an early convert from the ranks of the Calgary middle class.) And before the government released its committee report, he had another pamphlet in circulation. This was *The BNA Act and Social Credit*, a rebuttal to the constitutionalists who maintained that a province could never legally introduce the techniques of Social Credit.

The government released its report on Social Credit in June. Its 127 pages were filled with testimony, but only two sentences amounted to anything resembling a conclusion. One noted that "while the evidence disclosed the weakness of the present system and the necessity for controlled Social Credit, it did not offer any practicable plan ... under existing constitutional conditions." And the other proposed "a thorough study—first to arrive at a definitive objective, and second to get a clear idea of the obstacles," along with "the best method of procedure to secure results."

In other words, the UFA proposed to do nothing about Social Credit.

Of course, there was probably nothing the UFA government *could* do about Social Credit. As a party, it was already split into two rival factions: monetary reformists attracted to Social Credit, and a new rising group of agrarian socialists who had formed the Cooperative Commonwealth Federation (CCF) in 1933*. The UFA premier of Alberta, John Brownlee, was a corporate lawyer as frightened of socialism as he was of Social Credit; his government's investigation into Social Credit was a sop to one faction, and its conclusions a sop to the other.

By the end of June 1934, John Brownlee was a doomed man— and not only because his party was falling apart. While the government committee investigating Social Credit was still ruminating, he was found guilty of seduction in a civil suit brought against him by his secretary and her father. It was a sensational scandal that had been hanging over his head since the previous year, when charges

---

*In neighbouring Saskatchewan, in the face of organized federal opposition right from their beginnings, the CCF would eventually take power in 1944, to form the first socialist government in North America. The Canadian system of free medical care is their legacy.

were first laid under the Alberta Seduction Act. The secretary was awarded $10,000, and, strangely enough, her father $5000. Brownlee had to resign as Premier before the report on Social Credit was even released. (The Brownlee case went through many courts over the next three years before the Supreme Court of Canada confirmed the original decision and the award to the secretary, but reduced her father's award to nothing.)

At the same time, Brownlee's Minister of Public Works was sued for divorce by his wife, who named a correspondent to the suit, much to the delight of the Liberal opposition.

PORTRAIT OF EX-PREMIER JOHN BROWNLEE. NOT HANGING IN EDMONTON LEGISLATIVE BUILDING.

The Liberal party saw in the scandals a way to break the UFA; but their eagerness to attack the government on moral grounds served merely to demonstrate their own cynicism in public eyes. The Social Credit movement alone remained aloof from petty politicking and scandal-mongering—after all, it was not yet even a formal political party, and its leader was the morally impeccable William Aberhart.

The summer of 1934 was the Golden Age of the Social Credit study group: hundreds more of them sprang up all over the province, often within the local UFA membership. At the Calgary Stampede that July, fifty floats carried Social Credit banners. Aberhart was careful to target every interest group he could think of: trade unionists, women's organizations, young people, small businesspeople. He and Manning hit the road again, logging 2500 miles in July alone, making 39 speeches to more than 30,000 people. Their speeches were not overtly political; they took the form of "talks" designed to provide topics for the study groups: "The Woman's Outlook on Social Credit"; "Young People and Social Credit"; "Depression and War in Relation to Social Credit"; "Current Events and Social Credit."

The first "United Mammoth Basket Picnic" took place in a Calgary park: more than 3000 people attended to listen for hours to Aberhart and his selected speakers. The open air mass meeting became the preferred vehicle of the movement. Aberhart learned quickly to include small businesspeople in his organizing effort: ignored by the UFA and themselves suspicious of the mainline parties, shopkeepers and other entrepreneurs were happy to supply goods and services to the Social Crediters, who aways remembered to publish their names in programs, brochures and pamphlets.

Getting a Perspective:
The View from Mars

Well aware by now of the power of radio, and his own ability in the medium, Aberhart introduced amateur theatrics and a note of slapstick into his educational broadcasts. In the fall of '34, the Man from Mars made his first appearance on the Back to the Bible Hour, along with a Mr. Cant B. Dunn and a certain C.C. Heifer. The Man from Mars—in real life, Charles Wilmot, a railway worker who could improvise a suitably alien accent— was astonished every week by examples of great poverty existing in the midst

of plenty. Manning and Aberhart, in humourous debate with Mr. Dunn and Mr. Heifer, would try to illuminate earthly economics for the extra-terrestial, who would inevitably begin to wonder aloud why earthlings lacked the wisdom to adopt Social Credit techniques immediately.

As winter came on, Aberhart hinted more openly that people should be thinking Social Credit for the next election. At the same time, he began to vilify existing political parties as rotten to the core, led by men guilty of "fornication, graft and hypocrisy" who were merely "henchmen of high finance" offering nothing more than "splutterings, ramblings, prattlings and bologna" to the hapless citizens of the province. He asked in their stead for "One Hundred Honest Men" prepared to devote themselves to the reconstruction of the province. His listeners responded by nominating hundreds of upright citizens for the cause.

The UFA, meanwhile, was bleeding to death. From their 1921 peak of some 38,000 members, its rolls shrunk to about 10,000 by 1935. In January of that year they tried again to discredit Aberhart by inviting him to present his views at their convention, where a vote would be taken to accept or reject Social Credit once and for all. Aberhart responded with everything he had. The night before the debate, Manning hosted an on-air reception for UFA delegates that was broadcast all over the province. The Man from Mars was there, perplexed as usual, along with Mr. Cant B. Dunn, who now realized that Social Credit was the only answer. High school students dramatized the poverty and hard times in a moving skit; and Aberhart closed the evening with another resounding speech. The next day he gave a two-hour presentation to the UFA delegates, complete with diagrams and charts. His theme was the Just Price and the Basic Dividend; he closed with his by-now familiar analogy of the blood's circulation in the body.

The cross-examination took the rest of the day. UFA leaders battered away at Aberhart with some success, for the final vote defeated the Social Credit initiative by an undisclosed margin. But the government glee was short-lived, for within a few short weeks Aberhart was ready for an election. The Bible Institute organized a straw vote that indicated 93% of the population might be behind the movement. Aberhart put his formidable organizational talents to work, breaking the provincial constituencies down into zones each with its own local organization. He called for the first party convention in April, where, to no one's surprise, he was named leader of the party with the power to select his own candidates (with the advice of the local offices), and with the coy provision that he not be required to seek elected office himself.

The UFA, planning for a summer election, panicked when they realized, finally and too late, just how popular Aberhart was. In an embarrassing about-face they suddenly invited Major Douglas back to Alberta, for a fee of $5000.00, to advise them on a Social Credit plan for the province. The desperation and cynicism behind such a move was clear to everyone but the UFA leaders themselves.

Douglas, it should be remembered, had his hands full at this time with disgruntled Green Shirts unhappy with his plan to take Social Credit—unencumbered by candidates or an organized political party—into an English national election. When the UFA invitation arrived, he packed his golfclubs and caught the first boat out of Liverpool.

By now, though, Douglas knew that whatever his feelings about Aberhart might be, it was the Bible Institute brand of Social Credit, and none other, that had a chance for power in Alberta. Once arrived in Edmonton, he was careful not to attack Aberhart or his theories, despite the attempts of his hosts to maneuver him into a denunciation. He even sent Aberhart a letter stating that there was no substantive split between the two of them, and—ever aware of conspiracy—to be careful not to accept anything as the Major's word not signed by him.

Douglas got royal treatment from members of the UFA cabinet, who welcomed him into the highest echelons of the social and golfing life of the capital. He put ten days into a "First Interim Report"— a hefty document in which he took the position that Social Credit could possibly be implemented by a provincial government under the property and civil rights clause of the BNA Act. The report didn't mention Aberhart, but neither did it imply that Aberhart's Social Credit League represented false doctrine. He advised instead that any attempt to develop Social Credit in practice would be met by tremendous opposition from organized finance and big government. To prepare for this, he recommended a radio network bankrolled with foreign exchange—a strong propaganda system big enough to weather the storm ahead.

Douglas's report served only to strengthen Aberhart in his cause. The UFA, having screwed itself again, could only await the inevitable.

COME TO THE
BIG NORTHERN ALBERTA SOCIAL CREDIT PICNIC

(Grandstand, ring-toss games, hot-dog stands,
soft drink booths, sports, children's races)

PROGRAMME: MR. ABERHART gives Invocation; band plays
"*TELL ME THAT OLD, OLD STORY*"
—End of invocation; baritone sings "*OLD MAN RIVER*"

MAIN ACT: Mock horse-race between the 4 Parties, called
by MR. ABERHART.
(Social Credit comes first, Liberals 2nd, then Conservatives
and far back in the rear, the U.F.A.)
—After the race everyone sings: "*WHAT A FRIEND
WE HAVE IN JESUS*".

BIG FINISH: MR. ABERHART (tears in eyes) talks of the Depression;
the struggle of the deep-sea diver with the *devilfish*,
which is "analogous to ALBERTA'S struggle with the
great money octopus"- "*Let us strike then with all our
might at this hideous monster*... must have a government that would forget the worship of *MAMMON!*"
—Earth-shaking applause from 10,000 picnikers.

THE CLOSE: Hundreds will weep at the closing singing of
"*O GOD OUR HELP IN AGES PAST*".

(the U.F.A. can clean up the mess)

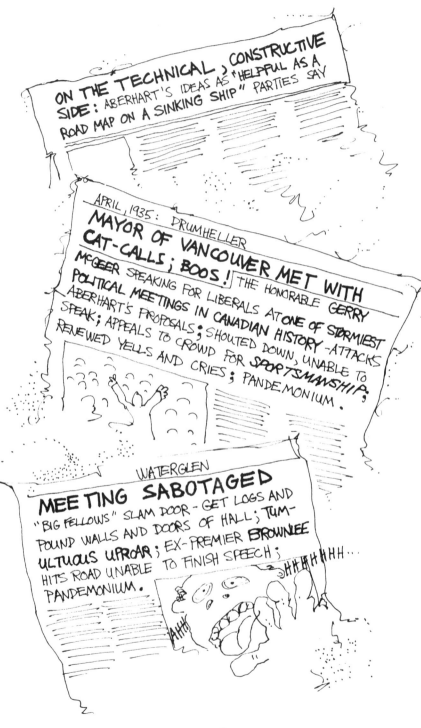

ON THE TECHNICAL, CONSTRUCTIVE SIDE: ABERHART'S IDEAS AS "HELPFUL AS A ROAD MAP ON A SINKING SHIP" PARTIES SAY

APRIL, 1935: DRUMHELLER

MAYOR OF VANCOUVER MET WITH CAT-CALLS; BOOS!

THE HONORABLE GERRY McGEER SPEAKING FOR LIBERALS AT ONE OF STORMIEST POLITICAL MEETINGS IN CANADIAN HISTORY - ATTACKS ABERHART'S PROPOSALS; SHOUTED DOWN, UNABLE TO SPEAK; APPEALS TO CROWD FOR SPORTSMANSHIP; RENEWED YELLS AND CRIES; PANDEMONIUM.

WATERGLEN

MEETING SABOTAGED

"BIG FELLOWS" SLAM DOOR - GET LOGS AND POUND WALLS AND DOORS OF HALL; TUM- ULTUOUS UPROAR; EX-PREMIER BROWNLEE HITS ROAD UNABLE TO FINISH SPEECH; PANDEMONIUM.

The inevitable happened on the 23rd of August, 1935: Voting Day. UFA candidates tried individually to win a public hearing, but only rarely got a chance to even finish a speech. The Liberals and Conservatives fared no better. It was a noisy campaign, filled with alarums in the night. Big business and banking interests rallied behind the Liberals, and called in their big gun Gerry McGeer, the colourful union-bashing mayor of Vancouver. (When McGeer landed his private plane in a field near Three Hills, an angry Socred farmer forced him back into the air.) The Edmonton Chamber of Commerce released a pamphlet entitled *The Dangers of Aberhart's Social Credit Proposals*, and banded together with other Chambers in the province to form the Economic Safety League. All this opposition only provided Aberhart with more targets: these "grafters, crooks, and worshippers of the Golden Calf" were in league with the "Fifty Bigshots,"; their principles were "those of the man who betrayed the Christ."

A touring UFA cabinet minister compared criticizing Social Credit to shooting peas at a warship.

On Election Day, more than 300,000 people went to the polls: 118,000 more than the election of 1930. And it was a complete rout: the Socreds pulled 56 of the 63 seats; the Liberals took five, the Conservatives two, and the hapless UFA: zero.

The first Social Credit government on the planet made headlines around the world. In London, John Hargrave assembled his Green Shirts in Threadneedle Street and marched seven times around the Bank of England. Frantic journalists searched everywhere for Major Douglas, who was out on his yacht. The Dean of Canterbury sent off an encomiastic telegram.

The UFA conceded the election at 10.30 pm. At the Bible Institute, an exhausted Aberhart slumped against his pulpit, as a chorus of party workers broke into "Oh God Our Help In Ages Past."

The next day Aberhart sent a cable to Douglas:

Victorious. When could you come?

ON MARS...

IN ENGLAND...

The EXPERIMENT

You don't have to know all about Social Credit before you vote for it. You don't have to understand electricity to make use of it, for you know that experts have to put the system in and all you have to is push the right button and you get light. So all you have to do about Social Credit is cast your ballot for it, and we'll get the experts to put the system in.

—William Aberhart

The new Social Credit government had two things to do right away: develop a practical plan for Social Credit, and get William Aberhart (who had personally abstained from the electoral fight) a seat in the Legislature.

A third problem was the imminent bankruptcy of the province. Aberhart hardly had time to name his Cabinet (which included 25-year-old Ernest Manning as Provincial Secretary and Acting Premier—the youngest cabinet minister in Canadian history) before he had to go to Ottawa to borrow money. There was some doubt the treasury could even meet its payroll.

Phones at the Bible Institute and the Legislative Buildings began to ring on the 24th. People wanted to know when to expect the Basic Dividend.

Before the election, Aberhart had asked the electorate for eighteen months in which to rally his experts and get the dividend scheme working. But his first problem was money. The Ottawa trip netted him only $2.5 million (he asked for $18 million). Immediate cash flow problems were so pressing that his first expert advisor was a man who had nothing to do with Social Credit: Montreal millionaire philanthropist Robert J. Magor, whose expertise lay in government cost-cutting. (Magor had been financial advisor to the Crown Colony of Newfoundland.)

Magor's appointment prompted Major Douglas, who was back in England but technically still on contract with the Alberta government, to withdraw his services. In a curt note, he suggested to Aberhart that "defeating the banks under the supervision of an agent of the banks seems to be dangerous." Aberhart kept the letter private, and sent Douglas a plea for sympathy avering that, given the province's economic troubles, the banks had to be appeased. "What we are anxious to have from you as our advisor," he wrote, "is the definite outline of some course in more or less detail, showing what steps you feel we ought to take when we begin to establish Social Credit." The Dean of Canterbury, on a Canadian tour at the time, visited Aberhart and reported back to Douglas that the Canadian Premier was vacillating and unsteady.

Welcome to
A Time of UNCERTAINTY & EXPECTATION
Main Speaker: The Dean of Canterbury
Topic: Vacillation & Unsteadiness
Entertainment: An attempt to borrow millions
from the Federal Government

It was time of uncertainty and expectation. Later in the fall, the Social Credit League ran candidates in the federal election, and won 17 seats, while Aberhart and his new Cabinet struggled to put together a program of legislation for the spring provincial session. Before the new year, he was forced to borrow another $3 million dollars from Ottawa, and began to hint publicly that eighteen months might not be enough time to get the dividend program working.

In November, the League parachuted Aberhart into office by acclamation in a by-election in High River-Okotoks.

The throne speech of 1936 promised only to introduce a bill "leading to the formulation and adoption of a plan based on the principles of Social Credit," and at the same time reassured worried business interests that "no ill-considered action of today will jeopardize the welfare of the future." The first Social Credit budget was an exercise in conventional economics: paring expenses, increasing mothers' allowances, increasing taxes on liquor, land and income; and imposition of a 2% sales tax. Only one bill referred to Social Credit directly; the Social Credit Measures Act, merely a piece of enabling legislation, authorized an investigation into monetary reform.

After all that fooferall, there were many who thought it was ...

Pretty Tame Stuff

First rumblings from the grassroots were not long in coming. In March of 1936 when the St. Paul chapter of the Social Credit League passed a resolution denouncing Aberhart for his "miserable failure to set up a new system." A wave of panic stories appeared in the press, based on rumours that people were taking their savings out of Alberta, and corporations were preparing to flee. (Just before the election, *Macleans*, a national news magazine representing the moneyed interests of central Canada, had branded Aberhart "the Hitler of Social Credit.")

Relations between Douglas and Aberhart continued to deteriorate. While Aberhart struggled to keep the province solvent on a day-to-day basis, Douglas encouraged him by telephone and telegraph to launch an attack on big finance, and to solve his debt problem by simply converting outstanding bond issues into "credit in Alberta"—a proposal that Aberhart either couldn't or wouldn't consider. Instead he made a plea for expert help, to which Douglas replied by recommending that he take on some of the old Open Minders who had opposed Aberhart in the struggle for Social Credit ascendency.

Increasing unrest within his own party finally obliged Aberhart to make his correspondence with Douglas public. He was losing face only a month after opening Parliament. On April 1st, his government defaulted on a bond issue and the province's credit rating plunged in world financial markets. In May the government cut interest rates on its bonds to 2.5%; in June, Alberta bonds were barred from the London Stock Exchange. Fighting for time,

Aberhart issued \$200,000 worth of "scrip money" in the form of Prosperity Certificates. These were merely promissory notes, redeemable in the future for money.

The scrip never caught on. Merchants refused to accept it, and Boards of Trade around the province denounced it. Aberhart's ministers even refused it as part of their pay.

Late in July 1936, the Social Credit caucus approved a program of citizen registration for the promised basic dividend. Amid the ensuing publicity, Ernest Manning predicted that six months would decide the dividend issue once and for all. Individual citizens were encouraged to sign "citizens' covenants," agreements by which the government would undertake to pay a monthly dividend, provided the citizen promised to abide by the rules of the yet to be created Credit House, and accept the dividends as currency. Similar covenants were submitted to merchants, wholesalers, and corporations.

The covenants proved to be a popular move; dissident elements in the party held their peace. The August session, one year after the election, brought a tendering of the first real Social Credit legislation: The Alberta Credit House Act promised to issue an unspecified basic dividend to all "covenanted, registered Albertans." Two Debt Adjustment Acts gave the government power to declare a debt moratorium; to declare interest owing on any loan made before 1932 uncollectable; and to limit loan interest—regardless of any agreements to the contrary—to five percent.

Here, finally, appeared to be the radical legislation so many had been waiting for. The eastern business community uttered a howl of rage. Their national magazine, *The Financial Post*, called it "a social and economic revolution commonly known as Communism. It strikes at the very roots of commerce, business and finance in a way which characterized the early stages of the Russian Revolution."

By October, the debt legislation was under attack in the courts, the Alberta Credit House Act was officially proclaimed, and the Bank of Canada refused Alberta a loan for $3.5 million. Aberhart announced provincial default on a further $1.25 million bond issue. Establishment political opposition began to organize itself behind a united front of anti-Socreds called the Peoples' League, while within Social Credit ranks, Aberhart's critics remained quiet–for a couple of months, anyway.

Late that December, Douglas sent Aberhart a cablegram warning him that John Hargrave, leader of the green-shirted Social Credit Party of Great Britain, had embarked for Alberta on his own initiative. (By now Douglas had disowned Hargrave and taken the green tartan away from him.) Hargrave arrived in Edmonton and found the press ready to hear him. Aberhart welcomed him cautiously and the Cabinet accepted Hargrave's offer of free technical advice. For some weeks he was shunted courteously from office to office, but being a man of action, soon began to chafe at the restraints under which the government was obviously labouring. "Alberta is like a kitten with a brick tied around its neck," he said to the press, "—that brick is the fictitious bank debt. You should cut away that burden ... there is no real difficulty in doing this. All it requires is a technical knowledge, plus courage."

An embarrassed cabinet was forced to quickly accept Hargrave's eleven-point plan for Alberta, which they took under advisement for another couple of weeks while Hargrave paced the hallways. Finally, after nearly two months of knocking around Edmonton, the green-shirted Social Credit leader had had enough. He invited reporters to his hotel room and complained at length about having to "deal with a preacher-schoolmaster personality," and compared the progress of Social Credit in Alberta to "a man stumbling along on a pitch-black night." Then he climbed onto a train and disappeared forever from the story of Social Credit in the western hemisphere. Hargrave's Eleven-Point Plan was never made public.

Aberhart was now estranged from all factions of British Social Credit. In February 1937, the Alberta Supreme Court declared his six-month old debt legislation unconstitutional. Aberhart launched an appeal and declared a moratorium on debts anyway. Then the court struck down his 1936 Act reducing the interest rate on provincial bonds. In the wake of these setbacks, a full-scale rebellion began to develop within party ranks, and dissatisfied party militants began to meet secretly in a hotel near the Legislature.

> (February 1937)
> (SECRET MEETING)
> (Dissatisfied Party Militants Only)
> (Tonight, Basement, Corona Hotel)
> (mum's the word)

In March, the government brought in a budget that made no mention of Social Credit and the militants began to attack Aberhart openly in the House. Overnight, the caucus split into two camps, the loyalists and the insurgents. The tension was enough to cause Aberhart to erect barricades across the corridor leading to the loyalists' meeting room. There were spies in both groups.

In power less than two years, Aberhart's government was perilously close to collapse. Half his caucus were with the insurgents. When he tried to choke off the budget debate (a debate prolonged by his own party members), the motion was defeated and he was forced to make terms with the militant wing of the party. As a result, the Social Credit Act was proclaimed, creating a new Social Credit Board charged with implementing Social Credit initiatives with a staff of anti-Aberhart insurgents. Board chairman G.L.MacLachlan was directed to sail for England immediately to see the Major, and to return with him or one of his "top experts."

Aberhart's compromise succeeded in stemming the insurgent tide but he was losing cabinet ministers at a frightening rate. By the end of April only three of his original ministers were still with him (besides Manning, who never wavered), and two of those were soon to go.

G.L. MacLachlan returned to Edmonton in June, having failed to convince Douglas to come back with him. But he bore in tow a man identified to journalists of the day as Douglas's "top political expert," George Frederic Powell. Another top expert—this one "financial"—L. Denis Byrne, was to follow in a couple of weeks.

George Frederic Powell's first job was to put the government back together again. He drew up a "Unity Pledge" and convinced both loyalists and insurgents to sign it as an act of good faith. The secret pledge (leaked to the press within days) began with a reiteration of the government mandate to institute a Basic Dividend of $25 a month—which was speciously noted to be "politically possible and therefore financially possible"—while binding the signer to uphold the Social Credit Board and its technicians, and to avoid "recriminations for the past and provocative utterances for the future." Powell demonstrated his diplomatic powers by convincing each side of the other's good faith. The insurgency faded away, with Aberhart committed to a more activist stance.

Throughout these times of tribulation, Ernest Manning contrived successfully to keep himself out of the public eye, and out of factional squabbles. During the period of the insurgency, he fell ill and took to his sickbed for its duration. His loyalty to Aberhart was never in question; but he was spared any direct confrontation with the insurgents.

When financial expert L. Denis Byrne got to town, the Social Credit Board began in earnest to design policy for the 1937 session, and on August 3rd launched a dramatic attack on the banks. A set of three related Acts put the banks under virtual control of the province: they were forbidden to operate without licenses for themselves and each of their employees, and, at the same time, denied access to the courts. The Lieutenant-Governor, whose imprimateur is necessary to bring new legislation into law, balked before signing, and asked the Attorney-General if he, as a lawyer, would affirm that the acts were within the power of the province. The A-G balked too, and Aberhart lost another cabinet minister.

In the next two weeks, under heavy pressure from the chartered banks, the federal government disallowed all three acts. Aberhart swore to keep fighting within legal channels, but in at least one public meeting enraged followers were heard to cry out, "Give us guns!"

Aberhart rewrote the disallowed legislation and brought it back to the Legislature along with a new Bank Taxation Act increasing provincial bank taxes by over 2000%. The Lieutenant- Governor "reserved" the new Acts for Ottawa approval and they went straight into the Supreme Court, where they languished until February of the following year.

At the same time, Aberhart foolishly turned on the big newspapers in an attempt to silence their growing criticism of his government. A bill called The Accurate News and Information Act empowered the chairman of the Social Credit Board to require the editor or publisher of any newspaper to name the source of any story and the writer of any editorial or article. It further empowered the Board to force any publisher or editor to publish "any statement furnished by the Social Credit Board Chairman which has for its object the correction or amplification of any statement relating to any policy or any activity of the Government."

The Press Gag Bill, as it became known overnight, garnered front-page coverage for Aberhart in newspapers across the country and around the world. Not surprisingly, he was most frequently compared to Hitler and Mussolini. (The Nazis in 1933 had enacted a Journalist's Law which made all journalists servants of the state.)

There was more trouble coming. When the '37 session ended on October 6, Douglas's political expert, George Frederic Powell, was arrested by Edmonton police and charged with criminal libel and counselling to murder. Powell had written for the Social Credit League a scurrilous leaflet entitled "Bankers' Toadies," which called for the extermination of that species of human being, listing nine of them by name. They included seven prominent corporate lawyers, an investment broker and the leader of the Conservative Party.

The Conservative Party leader laid the charges, and Powell was found guilty of publishing a defamatory libel. His sentence was six months at hard labour, and deportation.

A year earlier, The Bankers' Toadies episode might have consolidated Aberhart's supporters behind him; but it came too late. That same November, his own constituency turned on him with a petition for his recall. This was especially humiliating: recall legislation had been introduced in Aberhart's first legislative session; it was his only election promise that made it into law. Two-thirds of his electors were now trying to unseat him. Aberhart successfully questioned the legitimacy of some of the signatures on the petition, and was able to get a motion through repealing the Act, thereby managing to save his seat while losing considerable face.

The 1938 session opened up in February with the entire '37 legislation package still before the Supreme Court. Aberhart introduced new bills prohibiting foreclosures on farms and urban homes. These bills were still in debate when the Supreme Court announced its decision disallowing all the '37 Social Credit legislation including the Press Gag Bill.

Every one of Aberhart's Social Credit initiatives had now been torpedoed in Supreme Court. The only financial tool he had left was the default. And so, by unilateral act, his Social Credit government reduced the interest rate on its own debt, and over the next year defaulted on $12,000,000 in debt payments.

The federal government eventually threw out the 1938 debt legislation as well, but waited for the results of the 1938 Saskatchewan election before doing so. Social Credit had launched a big electoral drive in the neighbouring province, and the feds wanted to gauge public opinion before taking further action against Aberhart. The Saskatchewan election was decisive: Social Credit took only two seats, but the rising C.C.F. party took ten, and formed the official opposition.

The socialist C.C.F. had been organizing on the prairies for years, and their steadily increasing popularity would eventually provide a lever for the Socreds to hold onto power in Alberta despite the total failure of the Social Credit program.

In the meantime, Aberhart could do very little. In preparation for an election in 1939, he was reduced to announcing an Interim Program of watered-down Social Credit-like legislation mingled with a conventional "Buy Alberta" campaign. Branches of the Treasury were set up throughout the province, to offer deposit and loan programs much like conventional banks, but without the resources of the chartered institutions.

The treasury was also empowered to issue "transfer vouchers" (carefully not called "money", "credit" or even "social credit") to anyone doing business with them who purchased at least one-third of their supplies in Alberta. Transfer vouchers were the last gasp of "real" Social Credit practice: a 3% bonus which could be used as cash through Treasury Branches by other merchants willing to accept them in their Branch accounts. Like the earlier issue of scrip, the vouchers were boycotted by wholesalers, and the system never got off the ground. Once the Second World War got underway, the voucher system collided with federal rationing policy (geared, of course, to reducing consumption, not encouraging it) and in 1945 was abandoned altogether.

Aberhart was able to hold power through the 1940 election, but his party's majority became only a plurality: they held onto 36 seats, and the opposition took 21 (total seats in the House had been reduced by a general redistribution). Aberhart himself took a seat in Calgary without much trouble, but the only solid victory among his ranks went to Manning, who kept his Edmonton seat with a landslide.

World War II gave Alberta Socreds breathing space. With the whole country involved in the war effort, there was no room for arcane debate, monetary or political. The question of redistribution of credit could be shelved for the duration. War, after all, is the great consumer, easily able to absorb any amount of production.

Unemployment rates dropped; grain prices escalated; personal incomes increased. As the gloom of the Depression evaporated, William Aberhart saw the urgency of the Social Credit cause fade away in the public consciousness. For him it was a dispiriting time.

In 1941 the University of Alberta announced that it would award Aberhart an honorary doctorate of laws in recognition of his service to the cause of public education—an award not unmerited: Aberhart had always fought to maintain educational spending even at the height of the Depression. As Minister of Education he had developed an efficient system of rural school districts; and all his adult life maintained that higher education was the right of every citizen, not a privilege limited to the few.

But when the degree recommendation went before the university's Board of Governors for routine approval, it was rejected out of hand. In a vindictive unofficial statement, the Board said "Premier Aberhart's record was not one that could be approved by an institute of learning." The old man was humiliated once again.

In 1943, the Judicial Committee of the Privy Council in England finally laid to rest Aberhart's last Social Credit initiative: The Debt Adjustment Act. (The Privy Council was a fossilized remnant of the colonial government structure embedded in the BNA Act.) Early that year, Aberhart's health began to deteriorate noticeably, and while on vacation in Vancouver in June, he died in the hospital. His wife buried him there, telling the press he would have wanted it that way. "We were too unhappy in Alberta," she said.

Aberhart's Cabinet journeyed to Vancouver for the funeral. When they got back to Edmonton a special caucus took only an hour to choose a new leader. On July 3, 1943, Ernest Manning, 34 years old, became the youngest Premier in Canadian history.

135

The REVISIONIST

With the death of its prophet, and the end of the Depression, Social Credit in Alberta appeared to be on the wane. But Ernest Manning grasped opportunity where he could find it; and in 1944 he found it in the handy spectre of creeping socialism. The C.C.F. party had been organizing nationally for ten years; a 1943 Gallup Poll put it ahead of all other Canadian parties in popularity; and in 1944 the people of Saskatchewan put a C.C.F government into power—the first socialist government in North America, under the fiery leadership of Tommy Douglas.

"CREEPING SOCIALISM"

At the same time in Ontario, the C.C.F. swept in seemingly from nowhere, to become the official opposition. The whole country was talking socialism as it poured its resources into the war effort. In Alberta the C.C.F. was not yet a major factor politically, but Manning perceived correctly that Albertans were conscious of it, and moved quickly to re-orient the Social Credit party into direct confrontation with the socialist bogeyman.

His 1944 election platform was stripped of the old monetary policies; in their place he introduced the paranoid rhetoric of "free enterprise" and anti-socialism. The old enemies–banks and financiers—were displaced by the threat of "bureaucracy, regimentation and totalitarianism." Social Credit became overnight the friend of individualism and "sound business practice."

Manning retained the orthodox Social Credit position on the establishment Conservative and Liberal parties: they remained in his characterization corrupt powermongers working against the interests of the average citizen; with no long-range objectives or a social conscience, they lacked what he called "principle." Both Social Credit and the CCF, on the other hand, he perceived to be founded in Principle, with one essential difference between them: the socialists represented Unsound Principle, and Social Credit stood for Sound Principle. It was a simple analysis, much easier to grasp than the A+B Theorem, and required no experts to interpret it.

The new doctrine proved to be a brilliant strategic move: big business, never a friend to Social Credit in the past, was quick to embrace it. Major newspapers in Calgary and Edmonton began to print editorials favourable to the Socreds, and small business people who had grown wary of Aberhart's "funny money" policies began to consider Social Credit seriously once again. As a result, potential voter support for the Liberal-Conservative opposition began to drain away.

In 1944, Manning called an unexpected election (he still had a year left in his term) and the results more than justified his new strategy. The Liberal-Conservative coalition lost sixteen of their nineteen seats, and were effectively destroyed as a political force. The new CCF party, although taking second place in 31 ridings, won only in two. Manning regained all the ground lost in the 1940 election, and firmly established himself with a new mandate.

Social Credit hardliners were more than a little dismayed by the shift in policy, and dissident rumblings could soon be be heard emanating from the offices of the Social Credit Board, where the militant faction of the rank and file hung out.

The old Social Credit Board created by Aberhart in 1937 had become distanced from the government power centre, its purpose (to create the always-elusive Social Credit plan) overshadowed by the war effort and undermined by the Supreme Court rulings. The Board had evolved into a low-key propaganda agency, continuing a program of lectures on Social Credit theory along with a leaflet-and-pamphlet publishing program. In 1943 the one remaining Social Credit "expert," L. Denis Byrne, still on retainer to the board, began to encourage more study of Major Douglas's theoretical work. Later that year, the Board was able to report that it had uncovered a fund of evidence indicative of:

> A plot, world-wide in scope, deliberately engineered by a small number of ruthless International financiers to accomplish their objectives.

This insight into world conspiracy was lifted directly from the Major's published "research"; for, although the Social Credit movement in England had by now disintegrated into tiny particles, the Major had not let himself grow idle. Indeed, the evaporation of his movement led him to detect a major plot against his theories: a malignant conspiracy that by the late '30s had swollen to embrace international banking interests, all political parties, communists, socialists, freemasons, Pan-Germans, Pan-Americans, Zionists, and a large part of the Jewish population of the world.

Major Douglas had convinced himself that representatives of all those groups were locked in a secret cabal with one overriding intention: the general enslavement of the world (and of course the defeat of Social Credit theory). When the hardliners in Alberta began to weave this thread into their own educational programs, Social Credit began to take on a lunatic colouring not likely to help Manning build a power base, or even retain the allegiance of the voters.

At the same time, the not quite-so-extreme extremists were wondering out loud what had ever become of the Basic Dividend and the Just Price. Manning moved first to appease the grassroots by introducing one last piece of legislation resembling something like the old Social Credit: the 1946 Alberta Bill of Rights. Based on resolutions passed by the Social Credit League, the Bill offered a few guarantees filched from the socialists (free education, free medical care and a guaranteed income) along with a new Credit Commission empowered to license banks and to setup a "consolidated credit adjustment fund" from which to issue "credit deposits" (the Basic Dividend in sheep's clothing) to Alberta citizens.

But this was to be a constitutional bill, and contained a clause specifying that it would not be enacted until its validity had been verified by the Alberta Supreme Court (which eventually killed it). Party militants accused Manning of defeatism, and the Social Credit Board began writing confidential reports criticizing the government. Manning waited patiently for the Board to issue its 1947 report, which it published without first offering it to Manning for comments and suggestions (as had been the practise in the past). The report offered a reiteration of the world-plot thesis, while questioning the validity of the secret ballot and the desirability of political parties. Manning responded in caucus by condemning the Board for issuing an unauthorized report, the contents of which he said were totally unacceptable. He then challenged the caucus by introducing a resolution repudiating anti-semitism and racial or religious intolerance in any form (while at the same time affirming the party's loyalty to essential Social Credit doctrines). The motion passed, giving Manning the green light for ...

A Night of Long Knives

Heads began to roll in government back rooms, as Manning proceeded methodically into a bloodless purge. First he bled the Board by stripping it of its budget and educational and publishing functions. Then, one at a time, he squeezed resignations from those who didn't offer them. Last to go was L. Denis Byrne, and with him went Earl Ashley, sole remaining militant in the Cabinet.

The Douglasites fought back briefly, but weakly. They formed the Douglas Social Credit Council and held it together long enough to print a few documents accusing Manning of selling out to the conspiracy. But, like so many Douglasite factions before them, they soon faded into the background.

In the process of clearing the decks, Manning effectively stripped the Social Credit movement of its Depression-oriented ideology. During those stormy days, he must have wondered occasionally what he would substitute for it. Anti-socialism and Sound Principle alone weren't enough to keep him in power. He needed something on which to exercise that Sound Principle—something substantial.

And then, only a month after the purge, fate handed Ernest Manning the vehicle he needed. Near a small town called Leduc, only a few miles outside of Edmonton, Imperial Oil had for some time been quietly drilling little holes a mile into the earth. On February 13, 1947, one of them exploded, unleashing a geyser of greasy black stuff into the atmosphere. One of the drills had penetrated an underground sea.

For the next twenty years, the meaning of Social Credit in Alberta would be expressed in a single syllable. Oil.

The Leduc strike ushered in an epoch, known to historians as ...

. . .

The MANNING ERA

Social Credit in Alberta sprang to life in the middle of the Depression as a radical reform movement dedicated to the abolition of poverty in the midst of plenty. The wartime boom diminished the urgency of that mandate; the oil boom eliminated it almost entirely. The Leduc strike set off a corporate oil-rush that lasted until the late '70s, sucking hundreds of thousands of new immigrants into the province and irrevocably laying the basis for an urbanized, secular society completely out of touch with rural Christian roots of the Social Credit movement.

After 1947, the party political system in Alberta slipped gently into a coma that would last for twenty years. During that time, Manning and his Social Credit government achieved the status of natural phenomena; like the Saskatchewan River, they just kept rolling along, effortlessly washing away the opposition's puny sand castles every four or five years.

The A+B Theorem was replaced by a new and even simpler formula: money plus Manning. The money began pouring in in 1948 when Manning opened the doors to the giant U.S. oil corporations eager to stake claims for the black gold. The corporations sent in exploration and rigging crews, threw roads into the hinterland and started hiring the locals to do the work. By 1961, half the Alberta work force was involved in oil or oil-related work; by 1966, oil revenues from royalties and deposits supplied the cash for one-third of provincial expenditures.

Manicured corporate executives and fast-talking industrial promoters woke up the sleepy prairie cities of Edmonton and Calgary, bringing with them a brash macho style, a Texas drawl and, always, more Yankee dollars. Ownership of the Alberta economy shifted from Eastern Canadian and English hands to American ones. Its management fell to the capable Ernest Manning, devout and imperturbable guardian of the public purse.

The role of government, in Manning's eyes, was to maintain a climate favourable to business investors. Tax incentives, low royalties, minimal goverment intervention, and no buy-Alberta provisos—these were the constituents of a favourable climate. In return, the public got jobs (for a while) and the government enjoyed revenue source outside the tax base.

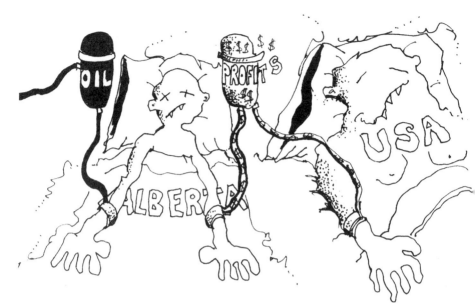

For two decades, Manning's free enterprise approach seemed to work. The market for oil improved yearly; unemployment was always low; per capita wages continued to grow, and government coffers filled up, as the oil companies sucked their profits out of the ground and took them back to Houston.

The government built things: roads, schools, hospitals, homes for the elderly. It even gave money away; before the 1955 election, Manning introduced direct cash payments to Alberta residents; known popularly as "oil dividends," they were an echo of the old Socred promise to end poverty through the redistribution of credit.

Manning had learned always to keep an eye on the CCF. Whenever the socialists developed an issue, he got out his wallet and nipped it in the bud. In the '50s the issue was care for the elderly; before the '55 election, Manning announced a plan to house more than 5000 pensioners. In the '60s it was Medicare, a socialist initia-

tive that Manning strongly opposed; the day before the '63 election he announced his own voluntary medical insurance program.

By 1964, Alberta was spending more per capita on education than any other province; and more than the national average on health and welfare. Social Credit became a government perceived by an most Albertans to be incapable of doing anything wrong. In twenty years, not a single scandal emerged to tarnish its record. Ernest Manning, who was referred to by everyone as "Mr. Manning,"—never as "Ernie"—continued his weekly broadcasts on the Bible Hour, delivering a new sermon every Sunday for a thousand Sundays.

Manning continued to support the old Social Credit dreams of monetary reform, but limited those aspirations to the national party, where the more militant of the old-line Socreds had found refuge. For a brief period in the '60s, he and W.A.C. Bennett from British Columbia threw their support behind Real Caouette, the zealous Socred firebrand from Quebec, in an eventually abortive attempt to install a Social Credit government in Ottawa.

At home, Manning steered clear of the old issues, and kept his attention on the work of the day. The oil boom seemed likely to last forever and there was always more money to spend. Toward the end of the '60s, in an effort to modernize the image of Social Credit (which was beginning to take on an antiquated air), he tried to inject a new ideological note into the movement, by introducing a concept he called "Human Resources Development," and proposing in a White Paper that private and public energies in the province be turned toward "facilitating the free and creative development of every human being in the province of Alberta." It was an ill-advised move. To the hard-line free enterprisers in his own party, Human Resources Development sounded like a socialist cover-up of welfare spending; to the opposition socialists, it sounded like Manning was proposing to treat human beings as a resource to be exploited, like oil or livestock.

It was a contradictory notion. Manning apparently intended by his proposal to achieve the old individualist goal—a society of individuals free from constraints—by intervening directly at the government level with government money. Only his terrific stature in the party kept his critics quiet; but many party members were uncomfortable with the idea, and when election time rolled around again, would be unable to explain it to the electorate.

Time might stand still for Social Credit in Alberta, but it wasn't waiting for anyone else. As the oil boom continued and the population grew, an urbanized society emerged. By the end of the '60s,

60% of Albertans lived in cities (in '47, an equal proportion lived in the country). Church-goers were in a minority, and the average age of the population was declining. The Social Credit League, content to grow old in power, remained oblivious to these changes; by 1965, their conventions were being compared by reporters to reunions of First World War veterans.

Manning fought the socialists all his life, perceiving his natural opposition to lie with them; but when the end came for Social Credit in Alberta, it came not from the left, but from the right, in the form of a smooth-talking, handsome young Tory named Peter Lougheed. Lougheed took the Tories into the '67 election on a vague platform that promised only to put new blood into management of the province; they pulled nearly a third of the vote. A year later, Ernest Manning announced his retirement from politics.

Manning's replacement was Harry Strom, a card-holding Socred since 1935. Strom proved unequal to the task of building party strength. Saddled with the Human Resources initiative that few in the party could accept, under fire from the Tories, who accused him and his party of being too old and tired, he bumbled good-naturedly through a term of office before going down to resounding defeat in 1971. The Tories took 49 seats, leaving the Socreds only 25.

As suddenly as they had come into power in 1935, Social Credit was out. Over the next few years, as it vanished rapidly into the past, Alberta Social Credit would become a memory cherished by fewer and fewer of its citizens.

The Manning era was a time of unfettered development and

profit-taking which Lougheed's Tories would try to sustain as long as possible. Not until the '8os, when the complexion of world oil markets begins drastically to change, would the wells stop pumping and the Americans begin leaving town. Only then would Albertans begin wondering where those profits went; where did the skilled technicians go; why is there nothing to replace the oil wells; why are Edmonton and Calgary turning into ghost towns?

Did Mr. Manning plan it this way? Surely not. Then just what was his plan, anyway?

The LAST FRONTIER

THE MOUNTAINOUS PROVINCE of British Columbia covers nearly a million square kilometres between the Rocky Mountains and the Pacific Ocean. Three quarters of its 2.75 million people live in its lower left hand corner; the remainder occupy towns and cities along river valleys in the interior, leaving the northern half of the province nearly unpopulated.

B.C. has never been a frontier dominated by small, individual enterprises, as were the Prairie provinces. (Agriculture has always been a small sector of the provincial economy.) Since the Hudson Bay Company's penetration into the area in the early 19th century in search of furs, B.C. remains a "company province," dotted by company-owned or company-based towns. Its economy is based in large-scale logging, mining, and fishing enterprises. It has always been a corporate frontier, rather than a wilderness of rugged individualism.

In 1857, the first gold rush brought thousands of fortune seekers into the in the B.C. interior (for a brief time, the remote town of Barkerville became the largest city north of San Francisco) but when an industrial pattern of economic and social organization emerged early in the 20th century, B.C. became an immense region of landless wageworkers, among whom developed a strong tradition of union-organizing.

Whereas on the Prairies the main social division lay between the farm world and the urban world with its link to eastern business interests, in B.C. it lay between the labour world and the world of middle class and big business.

B.C. joined the Dominion of Canada in 1871, with a population of 12,000 white and approximately 25,000 native Indians. At that time there were some 200 languages and dialects in use in the province; today, English predominates.

SEND ME YOUR HUDDLED CORPORATIONS, SHADY INVESTMENT DEALS, AND MOST IMPORTANT, THOSE MONOLITHIC OUT-RAGEOUS DEVELOPMENT SCHEMES FROM THE OTHER PLANETS.

146

The REALITY

British Columbia 1952–19??

1932

Welcome to the

DOUGLAS SOCIAL CREDIT STUDY GROUP

(of British Columbia)

Dress: Informal

Time: Off & On for the next few years

The Social Credit movement got off to a slower start in British Columbia than it had in neighbouring Alberta. About the same time William Aberhart was soaking up Major Douglas's ideas back in 1932, a newspaper reporter named Henry Torey was gathering friends into a Douglas Social Credit Group in Vancouver—a handful of people who met off and on over the next few years for informal discussion. In 1934 they achieved a brief prominence when Major Douglas passed through Vancouver on his first trip to Alberta. At a meeting sponsored by the Group and the Kiwanis Club, more than a thousand people turned out to hear Douglas, who was well-received by the press too. The Vancouver *Province* was especially impressed by the doughty Major, who spoke, as its reporter fondly put it, "in the deep intonations of a cultured Briton."

The provincial government was likewise impressed by those deep intonations. Premier Duff Pattullo invited Douglas to address the House, which was reported by the *Province* to be "deeply moved" by his monetary proposals, although it's more likely the government was relieved to hear the Major's assurance that Social Credit presented no threat to any existing political party.

1935

Welcome to the Formally Incorporated

SOCIAL CREDIT LEAGUE OF B.C.

(a result of the remarkable victory of Social Credit in Alberta)

After the Major's visit, membership in the Social Credit Group grew; its meetings began to attract sixty or seventy people a night. When Aberhart achieved his remarkable victory in Alberta in 1935, the Group formally incorporated itself as the Social Credit League of British Columbia, the official objectives of which were stated to be purely educational. Later the same year, when Alberta Social Crediters took 16 seats in the federal election, activists in the BC group began to organize politically.

Aberhart journeyed out to the coast to add his eighth of a ton to the B.C. movement, which patched together a platform combining mild reform with a $40 a month dividend. But the movement failed to catch on like it had in Alberta: in the 1937 election the League managed to pull in less than 1% of the vote. This failure eliminated Social Credit from the public arena, but didn't destroy it altogether. For the next fifteen years, Douglasism would remain alive and barely breathing in B.C., while it splintered into a myriad of tiny factions.

During the early years of World War II, the Social Credit flame was kept burning among a small group of dedicated Douglasites who formed themselves into a secret society called the Perfect Circle—its name meant to suggest the perfect circulation of money. Perfect Circle initiates (of whom there seems never to have been more than about thirty) recognized each other by tiny gold pins worn in their lapels. To achieve induction into the Circle, novices had to penetrate a maze of rooms, each offering two exits labelled with contradictory slogans (for example, "Credit belongs to the banks" and "Credit belongs to the public"). Choosing the exit with the correct slogan led the inductee into yet another room with two exits, and so on, until the end of the maze was achieved. An incorrect slogan led directly to the hallway. As Peer Paynter, an early Perfect Circler, explained, "If you got out into the hall, you had to do some more studying."

Over the next ten years, the light of Social Credit flickered on and off in other small coalescings of advocates: the United Democrats, led by an enthusiastic druggist; The Democratic Monetary Reform Organization, an unstable alliance of Aberhart followers and Douglasites; the Federation of Canadian Voters; the National Dividend Association; and the British Israelites, who believed the British people to be a lost tribe of Israel and espoused a biblical brand of economics that included the cancellation of all debt every seven years (a notion that would eventually make its way into the imagination of W.A.C. Bennett).

In 1944, the Social Credit Association of Canada (the national organization led by Solon Low of Alberta) felt optimistic enough about Social Credit prospects in B.C. to sponsor a provincial branch under the leadership of Major A.H. Jukes, DSO, OBE, late of the Ninth Ghurka Rifles of the India Army. Described by one historian as "an inveterate moustache twiddler," Jukes had been a charter member of Arthur Kitson's New Economic League in London. (See Part One.) He was a Douglasite opposed to large organizations of any kind, including political ones; as such he was an unlikely choice for leader, considering that the national association wanted Social Credit to fight another provincial election.

In the B.C. election of 1945, 16 Social Credit candidates culled from various factions took the field. But again, they had no grassroots organization. Opposition to the main-line parties centred almost entirely in the socialist Co-operative Commonwealth Federation (CCF) under Harold Winch. The CCF took 37% of the vote; the Liberal-Conservative coalition 56%; independents and other fringe groups nearly 7%; and the Socreds came up with less than one-half of 1%.

In the wake of another humiliating defeat, the Social Credit movement continued to splinter. Adherents obsessed by theories of an international Zionist conspiracy rallied together as the Union of Electors (never to be heard from again); while another equally tiny group, somewhat less esoterically inclined, coalesced around a Vancouver streetcar operator named Lyle Wicks.

Wicks claimed to have been introduced to Social Credit theory in 1944 by a fellow streetcar driver who said to him one day, "There is no reason why a man should have to stand fifteen minutes waiting for a bus. Why can't we have more buses? Social Credit would provide more buses."

Wicks tried to displace Jukes in the BC Branch of the Social Credit Association, but found himself blocked by a group of hard-line Douglasites firmly opposed to political organizing. With another dissatisfied Socred, he formed the BC Social Credit League in 1949. (Not the same as the by-then defunct Social Credit League of British Columbia). Wicks attracted support from the Alberta party, who by now had no use for the "orthodox" Jukes, and managed to recruit 400 members at his first convention. Wary of the lunatic fringe, he contrived to bring in people willing to play down Social Credit doctrine in public, and in the '49 election the League took 1.5% of the vote, without ever publicly mentioning the A+B Theorem or the National Dividend.

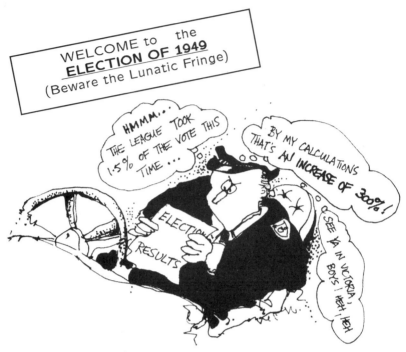

It was only 1.5%, but to the optimistic Wicks, that fraction represented a 300% increase over the last election. Things were looking up; the B.C. Social Credit League emerged as the only organized (if yet almost unheard) Social Credit voice left in the provincial movement. The fringe had been cut away, leaving a reasonably moderate, if small and inept, nucleus of dedicated movement workers. The Alberta Social Credit party, riding high after Ernest Manning's discovery of oil, began to take a serious interest in its sibling on the other side of the rockies. Serious interest meant serious money, and the Alberta party had lots of it. Money for offices, printing, postage, hall rentals, and a salary for a full-time organizer.

Peer Paynter got the organizing job. Coached by seasoned Alberta veterans, he began a fulltime recruiting program, setting up enclaves of supporters in towns and villages throughout the province, supplying them with literature and books of membership blanks. Door-to-door organizing went on for three years, and for the first time, Social Credit in B.C. took on the characteristics of a real grass-roots movement. By 1950, all it lacked was a credible leader.

Meanwhile, in the Back Benches ...

Since the '30s, the Liberal and Conservative parties had been hanging onto power in British Columbia only through increasingly shaky coalition governments opposed by an increasingly popular CCF, who had about a third of the popular vote by 1949. The coalition was an unstable entente weakened by patronage battles and power struggles that effectively isolated its own back benchers from any direct participation in power, and was always in danger of falling apart. It was an essentially moribund administration clearly on its last legs.

One of the noisier Conservative backbenchers was a hardware merchant named W.A.C Bennett, who had been sitting in the back row for ten years. A thorn in the side of the coalition government, which tried to keep him quarantined on the party fringe (he had twice run for the party leadership against the old-line machine boss Herbert Anscombe), Bennett had no qualms criticizing his own party, and was known to do so regularly, whether the subject be liquor laws, hospital insurance, coloured margarine, or political patronage.

W.A.C. Bennett had been in government for a long time, but never in a position of power. In 1951, he correctly perceived that the ruling coalition was doomed; furthermore, neither the Liberals nor his own Conservatives were capable of forming a government independently. If he were to have a political future, it would have to be outside the established party structure. The CCF, with its working class tradition and socialist philosophy, was becoming the only viable political structure in the province; but it could never provide a congenial home for a merchant-politician who believed all his life that "the finest music in the land is the ringing of cash registers."

W.A.C. BENNETT

He was the only man I ever knew who could get money from the rich and votes from the poor with the promise to protect them from each other."—Tommy Douglas, paraphrasing George Bernard Shaw

WILLIAM ANDREW CECIL BENNETT was born in 1900 in the village of Hastings, New Brunswick, with a caul (a membrane covering the face—believed by many to be a sign of future greatness). His father was a ne'er-do-well, rarely home and rarely employed. His Presbyterian mother brought up her five children herself, with the help of her relatives. Young Cecil quit school after grade nine to work full time in a hardware store in Saint John. As an apprentice merchant, he learned to keep books and produce balance sheets, as well as cost accounting and the intricacies of tariffs and customs duties. He joined the army when he reached seventeen and a half years of age, but the World War ended before he could be issued a uniform. His father, who had disappeared into the war, returned home in 1919, with a plan to go west under the aegis of the Soldier Settlement Board, and eighteen-year old Cecil decided to go with him. At a place called Teepee Creek, just inside the Alberta border in Peace River country, his father chose to settle on a small parcel of fertile land. Cecil stuck with him through the summer of 1919 before retreating to Edmonton, where he found a job as an order clerk in the local branch of Marshall Wells Ltd., the giant hardware firm. Apparently he never saw his father again.

...REFERRED TO BY SOME AS A "WINDMILL" WHEN SPEAKING IN PUBLIC AND ONE OF THE NOISIER CONSERVATIVE BACK-BENCHERS OF THE EARLY DAYS, I WAS IN ANY CASE A DEVOUT (IF SOMEWHAT SELF-RIGHTEOUS) CITIZEN, NEITHER PAR-TAKING OF SMOKE OR DRINK OR CONVERSATIONS ON LACK OF MONEY...

W.A.C. continued ...

His mother joined him in Edmonton unexpectedly, and after an unsuccessful attempt to reunite with her husband, set up housekeeping in Edmonton with Cecil, one of his sisters and his brother. As a young man Cecil adopted the blue serge suit that later became his trademark. He was active in the Presbyterian Church, and at one time considered entering the clergy. A devout if rather self-righteous citizen, he was an eager student of postive thinkers like Orisen Marden (a forerunner of Norman Vincent Peale). A non-smoker and a non-drinker, he lost his first girlfriend when he refused to take her to a public dance. He met May Richardson, his wife-to-be, in a young people's church group. He rose to assistant sales manager at Marshall Wells, before going into a hardware parnership with another man in Westlock, fifty miles north of Edmonton. The stock market crash of 1929, along with plummetting wheat prices, prompted him to sell out in 1930 and move to the Okanagan Valley in B.C. In Kelowna he bought out an existing hardware store worth $50,000 for $14,000, and the seeds of the Bennett Hardware chain were sown. In the mid-thirties he joined the Conservative party; by 1937 he was president of the Board of Trade. He won the Tory nomination in the provincial election of 1941, took the seat handily, and sat as a Conservative member for the next ten years (with a brief timeout for an abortive bid at a federal seat), biding his time.

Cecil Bennett was physically an awkward man: speaking in public he moved his body like a windmill; never an orator, he sputtered erratically when he spoke, but he loved verbal combat and he could handle hecklers adroitly. His pasted-on smile never left his face for thirty years. In school he had excelled at arithmetic; as a politician, his ability with figures surpassed Aberhart's: he could rattle off numbers almost endlessly, peppering an audience with budget details, projections, summaries, profit and loss statements, balance sheet figures, and statistics for any area of production in the province and much of the outside world.

...ONCE THE MISSUS TOOK ME TO SEE SOME ITALIAN OPERA – "LA TRAILER TRACTOR" OR "LA TRA LA LATVIA" OR SOMETHING, BUT I COULDN'T WAIT TO GET BACK HOME AND LISTEN TO SOME OF MY FAVORITE MUSIC!

CONTINUED ...

In March of 1951, Bennett rose in the house to announce his decision to withdraw from the coalition government, and to sit as an independent member. It was a move perceived in the press and among his constituents to be courageous, marking the fifty-one year old conservative as a principled and independent politician. One of his first letters of support was from Lyle Wicks, president of the B.C. Social Credit League; the two met privately a few weeks later to discuss the future of Social Credit in B.C.

Bennett was taking a calculated risk; if more unhappy coalitionists were to follow him across the floor, he might be in a good position to start another political party. But only one of his fellow backbenchers was willing to risk it. Tillie Rolston, Conservative member from Vancouver-Point Grey and an old friend of Bennett's, took the plunge later in the spring. It was a good time to take a stand: the government was floundering in the face of widespread public opposition to proposed increases in hospital insurance. A 205,000-signature petition opposing the increases had appeared in the legislature and the government refused to debate it. Bennett and Ralston had an issue ready-made on which to base their defections.

His defection from government brought Bennett into the limelight and for the next nine months, as a independent maverick, he railed away at the inept and corrupt coalition government.

In December of 1951, he took out membership in the Kelowna chapter of the B.C. Social Credit League. It was a move that surprised only the media, who were quick to accuse him of crass opportunism; in truth, it turned out to be a marriage of true minds.

Ernest Manning and the Alberta party, perceiving a power vacuum developing in B.C., had been spending their money well. All through 1951, they sent speakers into the B.C. hinterland in support of Peer Paynter's organizing efforts. In the small cities and towns of the interior they found the religious sectarians, the shopkeepers and farmers, the independent contractors and the unorganized workers they needed to form a grass roots movement.

The Social Credit position in the prosperous '50s was fundamentally no different than it had been twenty years earlier: rhetorically opposed to both "monopoly" and socialism, it attracted those in the disaffected centre who clung steadfastly to the virtues of 19th-century liberalism. Preaching good Christian government and free enterprise, the evangelical Socreds held up Alberta as a shining example of purity in business and government: the promised land achieved in our own time. "Not oil," one of their speakers told an enchanted audience, "but a good, honest Christian government has made Alberta. All you need for a government in B.C. is a dozen honest men. You are loaded with wealth. Why don't you keep some for yourself?" By the end of 1951, the B.C. Social Credit League boasted 3000 members; but among them were no experienced politicians, and no natural leader had risen up from the ranks. When W.A.C. Bennett joined it, the League was a body without a head and growing fast.

As an experienced merchant-politician with a high profile but no party, Bennett was himself like a head without a body while he remained an Independent in the legislature. Within the Social Credit League, Lyle Wicks and other B.C. Socreds (including Eric Martin, who joined the cause in the mid-40s) welcomed him excitedly, while others more closely connected to Ernest Manning and the Albertans saw in him a threat to their control over the B.C. movement.

Popular interest in Social Credit accelerated with Bennett's enrollment, and he quickly became a dynamic movement organizer, touring the small cities and towns of the Interior and setting up Social Credit cells wherever he went. He relied on a network of travelling salesmen for information and propaganda support. In the spring of 1952 membership in the League reached 8000. At the same time of course, Alberta Social Credit money kept pouring into the province, and high-profile Alberta Socreds like Orvis Kennedy and Solon Low toured B.C., while Ernest Manning harangued the Interior residents with his weekly Bible Hour.

WELCOME to the June 1952 ELECTION (a funny numbers game, introducing) The new Transferable Ballot!)

The Liberal-Conservative coalition government knew it was in trouble. Afraid that the CCF would win an election, they concocted a new voting mechanism called the transferable ballot: voters were to indicate their choice of candidate in order of preference, from first to last. If there was no clear winner with first choices, the second choices were to be counted, and so on, until a winner was found. The coalitionists were gambling that CCF voters (about a third of the population) would vote Liberal as a second choice; and that Conservative or Liberal voters would indicate the other coalitionist party as a second choice. The result would be a Liberal minority government, with the CCF shut out from power.

Social Credit voters were not taken into account in these calculations.

The election call came in April, 1952, and was set for June 12. The Socreds called a leadership convention and packed over a thousand delgates into a New Westminster highschool gymnasium. By this time, Tilly Rolston had joined the League, and announced that she would seek renomination as a Socred. This brought the number of experienced politicians in the movement to two. W.A.C. Bennett was ready to make a move for leadership, but he learned during the convention that many Alberta people were still against him. Trying to buy time, the Albertans pushed through a resolution calling for election of a campaign leader only: Social Credit being a "movement," it did not yet need a political leader. (This "non-political" stance was a central tenet of the movement. Instead of a platform, for example, the League proclaimed an election "program.")

Before allowing his name to stand as nominee for the campaign leadership, Bennett managed to get through a resolution allowing which allowed only *elected* Socreds to name their leader after the election. He took the occasion to assure the League of his Social Credit sincerity:

WELCOME to a MEETING of the "Headless Brigade from over the Mountains"

He then withdrew his name in favour of the Alberta choice for campaign leader: Reverend Ernest Hansell, the gnome-like leader of the sectarian Church of Nazarene. Hansell was a dyed-in-the-wool Socred of the old school, animated by a vision of world conspiracy and apocalypse. "There is a government more powerful than governments," he told his audience, "a great monetary power that knows no international boundaries. This is what we are attacking, and everyone who opposes Social Credit is either ignorant of that power or a party to it." (Hansell was a federal MP and saw the rise of Social Credit in B.C. as part of an overall attack on Ottawa and the eventual installation of Douglasite monetary reforms.)

Bennett's decision not to contest the campaign leadership kept the Alberta people in the League, and avoided a split in the ranks. So the party went into the election without a political leader, much to the amusement of the coalitionists, who called the Socreds "the headless brigade from over the mountains." But the League was not to be deterred from tumbling directly into the election. From all over the province, at hastily-gathered conventions, a motley collection of candidates was culled from among the disaffected middle class: ministers of the gospel, naturopaths, retailers, wholesalers, notary publics all leapt into the fray, to the sombre melody of "God Our Help In Ages Past."

The Socred program was the by-now classic mixture of anti-monopolism, political Christianity and business pragmatism. Touting the virtues of the Alberta example of "sound government," they promised a new world of small business and "individual enterprise" free from the scourge of monopoly and greedy politicians.

Throughout, the Socreds claimed to be above politics. As the Rev. Hansell put it:

> Social Credit is a great crusade for a way of life. It is a subject involving the destiny of the human race.

The Liberals and the Conservatives fought lame-duck campaigns, bitterly attacking each other and trying to stand "on the record." Convinced that their only real opposition lay with the CCF, they fulminated as always about the evils of socialism and prayed that the transferable ballot would somehow save them.

Only the CCF seemed to perceive a Socred threat; late in the campaign Harold Winch and his followers began to characterize the Socreds as anti-semites and extremist kooks. They exhorted voters to forego the multiple-choice ballot and to make only a first choice for the socialist candidate.

The polls closed at eight o'clock and election officials began the complex business of counting up the multiple choice ballots. A month later, when the results were finally collated, the CCF had 34.3% of the popular vote and 18 seats; the Socreds 30.2% of the popular vote and 19 seats. The Liberals and Conservatives, after fifty years of holding power in the province, were destroyed, with 6 and *four* seats respectively.

The transferable ballot annihilated the old-line parties, while succeeding in its secondary purpose of stopping the CCF. Polling results showed that the Socreds picked up a majority of second choices from voters whose first choice was Liberal or Conservative; as well, they picked up a surprising number of second choices from CCF voters. Socred strength lay in the hinterland of the province where they won 16 of their 19 seats. Only three Vancouver seats fell to them, and none on Vancouver Island.

Giddy from their unexpected success, the elected Socreds met hastily to choose a leader. There was little doubt about the outcome: Rev. Hansell had his bags packed and was on his way back to Alberta when the meeting started. W.A.C. Bennett, the only seasoned politician among them, won on the first ballot. (He was opposed by Phil Gaglardi, Pentecostal minister from Kamloops, Thomas Irwin, a farmer from Delta, and the long-suffering Peer Paynter, who had been narrowly defeated in Revelstoke.)

Bennett spoke to the press that night:

> Social Credit is just the opposite of funny money ... with God's help we'll do our best. Go easy on the monetary stuff. Remember it doesn't concern us now.

It was up to the Lieutenant-Governor to invite either the CCF or the Socreds to form a minority government. Harold Winch tried to make a case for the CCF, who had a larger portion of the popular vote, and many years of parliamentary experience, but the Lieutenant-Governor—no friend of socialism—took counsel with the Liberals and Conservatives, and on August 1, 1952, invited W.A.C. Bennett and his Socreds to form the new government.

Bennett was ready for the invitation, with a Cabinet quickly patched together from his ingenue caucus. Tilly Rolston, 65 years old and the only other politician in caucus, was assigned the Education portfolio; Lyle Wicks got Labour; and Eric Martin Health and Welfare. Other caucus members who made it onto the front bench were all newcomers to both Social Credit and the Legislature: among those who would make names for themselves were Robert Sommers, a school teacher whose hobby was fighting forest fires (he got Lands Forests and Mines) and the Reverend P.A. Gaglardi, who got Public Works.

There being no lawyers at hand to fill the Attorney-General's position, Bennett went outside the party, and scooped up Robert Bonner, a young Conservative lawyer without a seat; and for Finance Minister, he turned to an old crony, Einar Gunderson, the accountant who handled Bennett's hardware chain. Gunderson, long-time Liberal, had valuable connections in big business, and would for some time be the only link between the new government and the halls of the exclusive country and dinner clubs of the powerful. Ironically, Gunderson had fled the civil service in Alberta in 1935, when Aberhart took power. Seventeen years later, the Alberta example seemed to have calmed his fears.

Old-time Socreds looked askance on the acquisition of these two establishment figures, but Bennett soothed their fears by referring to their much-needed expertise, and reminding everyone that Social Credit was a movement not tainted by political partisanship.

After the swearing-in ceremony, the new cabinet retreated to Bennett's hotel room to celebrate. There was Ovaltine for everyone. It was time to begin ...

The BC Experiment

When Social Credit took power in B.C. the province was in the midst of an economic boom: foreign investment in the resource industries was accelerating rapidly; unemployment was almost nil; wages were rising and government revenues had reached an all-time high. Construction was booming. Shell Oil was building refineries in Burnaby and a trans-mountain pipeline was under construction, slated to begin pouring Alberta oil into the Vancouver suburb by fall of 1953.

The forest industry, hub of the provincial economy, was expanding at a terrific rate. In 1952, American investment in the industry was over 50%, and the U.S. was buying more than 80% of its lumber exports. In just six years the production of pulp and paper had nearly doubled to nearly a million tons.

There was plenty of money around, and lots more where it came from. The old Depression dreams of monetary reform were hardly relevant to the boom-time fifties. W.A.C. Bennett claimed to have studied the A+B Theorem (in fact, in his later years, he maintained that he understood it better than anyone else in the movement) and was content to leave its implications to the militant purists while he pursued a trail already marked out by Ernest Manning in Alberta. Never a bookish man, Bennett developed working definitions of

Social Credit as he went along. In 1953, he likened Social Credit to driving a car on a hilly road:

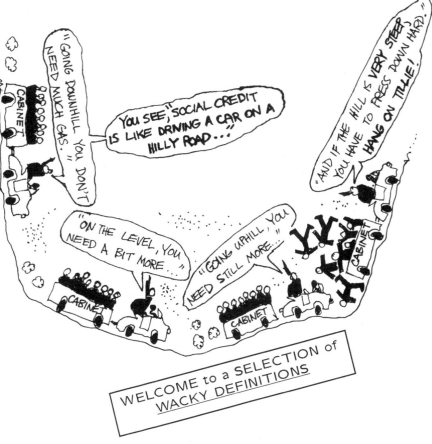

When the Archbishop of Canterbury, an old Douglasite, visited the province in 1954 and asked the Premier what Social Credit meant to him, Bennett solemnly quoted St. Paul's remarks on Christianity:

> Unto the Jews, it is a stumbling block; unto the Greeks it is foolishness; but we know unto millions of people it is life eternal.

By 1960, he would be able to say to a reporter:

> Social Credit is the opposite of socialism.

Whenever questioned about political accountablity or modern democracy, Bennett had a stock answer:

> True direct democracy is that the elected must govern, and

must not be governed by the electors. Unless the elected govern, you have a dictatorship. If the electors govern, you have anarchy ... In other words, people in a democratic way select people to do a job. Then they must have authority to do a job and they must boldly do that job, and they must not ask questions and have royal commissions all the time.

Seventeen years earlier, William Aberhart had toyed briefly with a populist system of direct accountablity and had been nearly unseated by it. The pragmatic Bennett was not about to make the same mistake.

Once in office, Bennett moved quickly to dilute the militant presence in the League membership by opening its doors to disaffected Liberals and Tories, who, sensing which way the wind was blowing, began to join the Socreds in increasing numbers. The League presidency fell to Bennett's man, John Perdue, who elbowed the hapless Peer Paynter out of the way for the job. To gain direct control over a political slush fund, Bennett installed Einar Gunderson as head of the newly-formed B.C. Free Enterprise Educational Association, a separate body charged with collecting money for election expenses, and to finance "a certain amount of sub-rosa educational propaganda on behalf of free enterprise apart from politics."

"A DAY AT WACKY'S OFFICE..."

169

Bennett moved quickly to make hay with voters as well. Wary of calling the Legislature too soon, he introduced his untrained Cabinet to the intricacies of government by order-in-council for the first eight months of their tenure. The first of these orders-in-council authorized payment of $10,000 to the Nicola Grasshopper Committee to help exterminate pests. Hundreds more followed. Cabinet ministers spread out over the province, carrying the free-enterprise gospel to Boards of Trade and Chambers of Commerce, who were promised roads, bridges, and contracts. In a weird kind of post-election campaign, Bennett made speeches around the province, reassuring businessmen that Social Credit would not restrict its favours to "only a few businessmen and industrialists," but would look after the needs of the "little man." In December, John Perdue made the political nature of these promises clear when he explained to a CBC interviewer the function of the Social Credit League in the new government:

> If a group finds in its area need for government assistance for a road or if a small logger wants to get a piece of timber, they make representation to the local Social Credit unit ... then you

see, how any individual can voice his desires and they can be passed almost immediately to the government.

In November, Bennett parachuted Robert Bonner and Einar Gunderson into the rural ridings of Similkameen and Columbia, where the citizens were entertained by the spectacle of two city slickers wooing the locals. But the wooing was powerful stuff: hundreds of promised miles of pavement, big dams, and the complete hydro-electrification of the entire Columbia River Valley. Bonner at one point promised cheaper long distance telephone rates, not knowing that there was only one phone in the local community. But the locals loved it all, and voted in Bennett's metro heavyweights with bigger majorities than the small-time Socreds who had stepped aside for them garnered in the June election.

Bennett travelled to Edmonton in December to meet with Ernie Manning. This can be seen as an historical event: as one of Bennett's biographers put it, "the first time that two heads of Social Credit governments had ever conferred." Along with the mutual flatteries such a meeting can be expected to produce, emerged an indication of Social Credit territorial ambition: a joint proposal for the annexation of the Yukon and part of the Northwest Territories.

Bennett led his neophytes into the Legislature on February 3, 1953. After a mild throne speech (prepared by Bennett) referring vaguely to "certain measures of considerable importance," opposition members rose to the traditional debate. But the entire Social

FEB. 3 1953
Welcome Bennett Neophytes
into the Legislature
Topic: Certain Measures
of Considerable Importance
(Please observe a 10-day silence out of respect
for all the dumb things we might say if we don't)

Credit caucus remained mute. Bennett had instructed his people well: rather than make fools of themselves answering the inevitable charges, not a single Socred said a word for the next ten days as each opposition MLA stood in turn to harangue them in a fruitless attempt to evoke a response. When they had all had their say, the urbane Robert Bonner delivered a single Socred response.

Einar Gunderson brought in an unremarkable budget that offered a few minor personal tax reductions, a new natural resource tax on logging company profits, and an increase in the mining tax and the tax on leased timber land. The logging and mining company PR men ran to the press, wailing about the end of freedom in the province, the inevitable "flight of capital" that would ensue on the heels of the draconian resource taxes.

Big business and the Socreds had not yet come to terms with each other. But in the meantime, the electorate could see the feisty populist party as unafraid of the corporate interests.

B.C. SCHOOLS ACCUSED OF BREEDING "THIEVES, ROBBERS, DOPE ADDICTS AND PROSTITUTES"!
TILLEY ROLSTON HEARD TO YEARN ALOUD FOR "THE DAYS OF THE LITTLE RED SCHOOL-HOUSE AND THE ROBUST FRONTIER"

The ensuing budget debate offered Socred caucus members their first opportunity to speak in the legislature. J.A. Reid, from Salmon Arm, used his maiden speech to attack the educational system, which he said was poisoning children's minds with immoral textbooks reflecting socialist tendencies. He read a letter from a constituent who claimed that B.C. schools were breeding theives, robbers, dope addicts and prostitutes. Tilly Rolston, the new Education Minister, yearned aloud for the days of the Little Red Schoolhouse and the robust frontier. Phil Gaglardi, the Kamloops preacher, reminded the legislature that he was a minister not only of the Crown, but also of the King of Kings (and queens):

In this little fella, you'll find lotsa faults and I'll make lotsa mistakes, but with the help of God, I'll do my level best for British Columbia.

At another point, accused by a heckler of lying, he responded:

Mr. Speaker, if I'm telling a lie, it's only because I'm telling the truth.

The session lasted for seven weeks, until the opposition were forced to combine forces and defeat the government on a proposed revision to school and municipal financing. This suited Bennett well: his neophytes had had a chance to get their feet wet, and he had a political case to bring to an election: the "people's government" was being obstructed by a disruptive opposition. Harold Winch of the CCF went to the Lieutenant Governor and tried vainly to convince him the socialists could form a government instead. But the CCF had, as ever, few friends in Government House.

The Liberals and Conservatives ran hysterical campaigns against Socialists and Socreds. The Tories enthusiastically branded the Socreds as socialists and fascists at the same time and ludicrously compared Bennett to Hitler. The Liberals denounced the Socreds as a gang of radical McCarthyites opposed to the United Nations, Jews, Liberals, labour, education, social security, free enterprise and parliament. At the same time they painted lurid pictures of the evils of socialist life under the CCF, and tried to maintain a place in the centre for themselves.

The CCF tried to maintain a reasonable demeanour in the '53 campaign by playing down socialist themes and emphasizing their Christian roots. But the Christian element in politics was on the wane; the Socreds had begun to eliminate it from their rhetoric as Social Credit moved into the secular phase in which it remains today.

Bennett took his party into the election with a simple seven-syllable slogan:

Social Credit or Chaos!

Bennett promoted his party as a responsible people's movement, "not a movement of cranks, not a funny-money movement," and promised lots of Alberta-style benefits: "Social Credit dividends—in hospital insurance, premium reductions, slashing of the public debt, reductions in sales tax and car licenses." At the same time, there would be no tinkering with the economic system. Whenever the question of the old monetary theories came up, Bennett trotted out the ponderously respectable Einar Gunderson to allay fears of an Aberhart revival.

Speaking directly to the middle-class, Bennett tirelessly repeated the populist formula of free enterprise:

> We are a people's movement, and oppose equally strongly the forces of monopolies and forces of socialism!

The '53 election brought the Socreds the majority they needed: 28 seats of a 48-seat House. (The CCF took 14, the Liberals 4, and the Conservatives 1.) It was a remarkable victory; four years earlier, the Socreds had mustered a mere 1.5% of the popular vote. Bennett was jubilant. In his first address to the province, he promised to unleash unparalled development of the "wealth of mineral, forest, oil, natural gas, and potential hydroelectric resources which constitute the last economic frontier of North America."

The only sour note for the Socreds in the 53 election was the defeat of Tilly Rolston and Einar Gunderson. Rolston could be replaced, but Bennett desperately wanted his accountant in the Finance portfolio. But Gunderson wasn't a politician at heart, and he lost again in an embarrassing by-election that fall. Relegated finally to financial advisor, he kept the job of party bagman, and Bennett himself took the Finance portfolio.

WELL, GUNDERSON, YOU TRIED TO GAIN THE FINANCE PORTFOLIO BUT NOBODY LIKES YOU, BUT I DO, SO HERE. YOU CAN CARRY THE MONEY.

In their first Parliamentary session, the Socreds eliminated or reduced minor taxes on children's clothing and shoes, liquor, meals and amusements; reduced car registration fees and increased the bonus to old age pensioners. Bennett solved the thorny question of hospital insurance in typically unorthodox fashion by sidestepping the question of compulsory or voluntary participation altogether. He added 2% to the sales tax to pay for the program, and simply abolished premiums entirely. An astonished CCF opposition could only acquiesce (free medical care was the basis of their whole platform), while the big city newspapers, still afraid of Social Credit, screamed "socialism." Bennett, ever smiling, claimed that the program was still voluntary; no one was being forced to accept the insurance; and meanwhile the direct burden on lower income groups was actually reduced.

Having thus buttressed his party's incipient populist reputation, Bennett promised to "spare no effort toward the attainment of British Columbia's manifest destiny," and the year 1954 became the first of ...

The PAVEMENT YEARS

Bennett, taking his cue from Ernest Manning in Alberta, made it his first priority to create the much-to-be-desired "favourable climate" in which foreign investment dollars might take root. At the same time, it was important to his sense of bottom-line bookkeeping that the government maintain a pay-as-you-go fiscal policy. Soon after the '53 election he incorporated the Toll Bridges and Highways Authority, a Crown corporation empowered to build highways, bridges and ferries, and borrow the money needed to do it. The government, while guaranteeing the Toll Authority's debts, was thereby spared the problem of showing those debts on its own books.

The Reverend Phil Gaglardi got the newly created Highways portfolio. The feisty Pentecostal brought a special flair to road construction. As bulldozers tore through great reaches of the province, he sped from town to town, cutting ribbons on bridges and pieces of pavement, never forgetting to thank "The Man upstairs" for allowing prosperity to come to B.C, or, at times, providing good weather for the ceremonies. His casual relationship with his Maker bespoke a casual relationship to other proprieties as well; he quickly developed a pleasing notoriety for reckless driving, accumulating an array of speeding tickets from uncooperative RCMP officers (one of whom he described as "a punk") as he sortied through the province at 70 miles an hour and more.

Gaglardi's rough-and-ready approach to politics was in keeping with the youthful, devil-may-care spirit of free enterprise that permeated the province in the '50s. His disregard for "rules" endeared him to a public excited and pleased to be part of the last frontier. In 1958, he opened a lavish new Calvary Temple in Kamloops, the cost of which was born in part by a number of devout road builders. When the *Vancouver Sun* suggested conflict of interest, W.A.C. rushed to Gaglardi's defense (for the first, but not the last time), with a swift denunciation of the paper's "smearing attack on Christian churches" and a loud touting of "one of the finest men British Columbia has produced ... this man who has buses to drive children to Sunday-school even if they aren't members of his Church!"

On the question of natural resources, Gaglardi summed up the party position when he said:

God put the coal there for our use, so let's dig it up!

"LATE ONE NIGHT IN THE ATTIC OF THE PARLIAMENT BUILDINGS IN VICTORIA, WACKY BENNETT BENDS THE EAR OF TINY PHIL GAGLARDI, HIS MINISTER OF HIGHWAYS..."

As the asphalt flowed and shining bridges began to cross rivers and lakes throughout B.C., contractors got contracts, workers got temporary jobs, and real estate speculators watched their property values escalate along rights-of-way.

Highways were the homegrown, high profile sign of prosperity. The province bristled with "Sorry for the Inconvenience Signs" bearing Phil Gaglardi's signature, a visible emblem of the heat of progress progessing.

At the same time, B.C.'s resource industries, which were already booming—world demand for raw materials being at an all-time high—seemed to boom even more as Bennett opened up the province to big mining and logging firms, finally putting to rest any fears big capitalists might be harbouring against Social Credit in B.C.

As early as the end of 1954, control of timber rights in the province had been consolidated among a handful big firms: in 1949, 58 firms held half the timber licences in the province and 2800 firms held the other half; in 1954, nine firms held nearly 80% of the total licensed acreage.

Independent contractors were being pushed out of the forests by a licensing system preferential to a few huge corporations. But at the same, employment levels in the forest remained high, and the voters were happy. The forest giants were happy too, and Einar Gunderson was free to call them up any time, on behalf of the Socreds' rapidly accumulating Free Enterprise slush fund.

Bennett was convinced that the enormous mineral and forest resources of the north and the magnificent river system were the key to prosperity, no matter who took the profits out of them.

Bennett's used quasi-independent Crown corporations to bear the cost of creating access into the hinterland, while at the same time protecting government ledgers from red ink. Then, with the infrastructure in place, Investment—that elusive panacea— attracted by the favourable climate, could then be expected to step in to create wealth for all.

The essence of the Social Credit solution was still intact 35 years after Major Douglas first proposed to alter the money system. That solution postulates quite simply that if we create the appropriate conditions—whatever they might be—we can expect Utopia to occur as a natural consequence.* In this respect, then, W.A.C. Bennett remained as dedicated an idealist as were his forebears in England and Alberta. His dream was, in a phrase, a dream of ...

BOOM Without END

---

*This is an ethical position not unlike that of the Marahishi Mahesh Yogi, who maintains that world peace will ensue once one percent of the world's population meditate at the same time.

To fulfill that dream, Bennett was prepared to take risks, and, when necessary, drastic action. The Pacific Great Eastern Railway was his first risky challenge. A political football since 1912, the PGE by the '50s was an anachronism: a rail link between the village of Squamish in the south and the small town of Quesnel in the middle of the province. It went from nowhere to nowhere, and owed the government—which, as its only creditor, had financed it all these years—$150 million. In 1954, in a dramatic gesture reminiscent of Aberhart's default on the Alberta debt, Bennett wiped out the PGE debt by a stroke of the pen, and, in a special act, empowered the railway to incur debt independently of the government. At the same time, the government purchased $60 million worth of PGE stock.

Small business people were shocked by the move. Writing off $150 million in receivables seemed, to say the least, unbusinesslike. Buying into the debtor operation with another $60 million seemed unreasonable as well. Bennett assured doubters of his good intentions by appointing himself (as president) and bagman Einar Gunderson to the PGE board of directors.

Bennett wanted the PGE because it was a transportation line that could (hypothetically) go where no highways would ever go: into the apparently unpopulated wilderness of the north.

Bennett applied his accounting technique to a program of school construction as well, by empowering school districts to borrow money directly and thereby to assume liabilities themselves. Accused by the press of juggling the books, and merely changing the name of the provincial debt, Bennett remained imperturbable, tirelessly repeating his pet phrases, "pay-as-you-go," and "debt-free." In an unprecedented wave of government spending, he was succeeding in his primary purpose, which was to put a bulldozer within sight of every voter. The public image of the pudgy politician began to take on a rather unlikely macho colouring. Venerable Socreds could be overheard uttering remarks like, "he's the type that chews nails and spits rust," and "Rome wasn't built in a day, but it might have been if our Premier'd been in charge."

WELCOME TO THE
Labour Relation Act of 1954
(We'll call it Bill 53—which is
shorter than "Union-Buster")

In the 1954 session, Social Credit turned its attention to organized labour, bringing in a new Labour Relations Act. Bill 28 brought industrial relations further into the political sphere, by shifting the power of the Labour Relations Board to the Minister of Labour and the courts. The Minister was empowered to appoint conciliation officers and mediation boards, and refer strikes to the Supreme Court, whose judges were in turn empowered to declare null and void the collective agreement, check-off and certification of unions judged to be striking illegally.

By pulling industrial relations directly into the political arena, the Socreds claimed to be protecting workers from their own leaders, who were relegated the role of political villains conspiring against progress. The move satisfied Socred back-benchers as well, who thought unions were perpetuating "undeserved luxury living."

1955-56
Welcome to the
HONEST BOB SOMMERS AFFAIR
Entertainment: Malignant Conspiracy
Special Event: A Snap Election
Special Prizes: $28-Dollar Social Dividends
Join the Fun!
Bribes for Everyone!

The Socred machine was developing at a break-neck pace in 1955 when Liberal MLA Gordon Gibson, who spoke for the small logging interests, charged in the legislature that Robert Sommers, Minister of Lands Forests and Mines, had been unduly influenced in his granting of timber licenses. In the uproar that ensued, the government hastily appointed a one-man commission to clear Sommers of the ensuing bribery charges, which it did in short order. But opposition members were unwilling to let the case die, and the Attorney-General was forced to hand the matter to the RCMP early in 1955.

With the credibility of his government at stake, and Bob Sommers complaining angrily of a diabolical conspiracy against him, W.A.C. Bennett stormed into the fray by issuing an election call before the RCMP report could be made public. The '56 campaign was a bitter one. The opposition parties tried to make a major issue out of the unresolved Sommers case, while Bennett stuck to the position that Social Credit was not a political movement, and urged voters to endorse "Progress—Not Politics."

The '56 Social Credit budget featured a new kind of "social dividend" aimed directly at the middle-class voter: a $28 tax remission for each homeowner in the province. The homeowner grant, which would become a standard vote-buying ploy in many provinces, was in fact simply a re-routing of funds earmarked for municipalities. Administrative costs for distributing the grants were borne by the municipalities, while the provincial government posed as munificent benefactor. It was a popular move. An exuberant Cabinet minister, perhaps not having scrutinized the A+B Theorem in close detail, proudly proclaimed, "We can see here the basis of Social Credit and the payment of the dividend!"

Compelled occasionally to comment on the Sommers affair, Bennett sympathized publicly with the plight of his colleague, who was running an ardent campaign as "Honest Bob" in Rossland. Referring the case to "the highest court in the land"—the voters— Bennett lashed out against the press who insisted on making a case of the affair. Purple with rage, he made a straw man out of Don Cromie, owner of the *Vancouver Sun*, maintaining that the issue was "not between political parties, but whether Cromie, this newspaper baron, is trying to set up a super government over the public representatives. I call upon all citizens of our province to rise up and support Social Credit candidates against this newspaper baron's dictatorship!"

More than 45% of the electorate did, in the event, rise up, and brought the Socreds back in with a clear majority: 39 members were returned to government in another remarkable victory. "We fought not only four other parties," chortled the Premier, "but the Canadian Broadcasting Corporation and majority of the metropolitan press." Inspired with hyperbole, he hailed the election as:

> The greatest victory for the ordinary people since the Magna Carta!

Honest Bob Sommers, acquitted by the voters, was nevertheless arrested in November of 1957, and after a lengthy trial, convicted of bribery and conspiracy and sentenced to five years in jail.

The Sommers affair stirred up trouble among Social Credit back benchers, some of whom had felt their loyalty severely shaken by the sensational trial. W.B. Carter of Pentiction, opponent of high taxes and fair-employment legislation, attacked his own government as "typical of socialistic, even communistic, administration"; and MLA Percy Young began making incoherent speeches about Zionists, who were apparently threatening to destroy Social Credit.

At about the same time, B.C.'s resource economy took a sudden nosedive; despite free enterprise rhetoric about the "favourable climate," investment in the province dropped as export sales fell, unemployment started going up and government revenues began to fall. (An economy so completed based in primary resource extraction is, of course, highly vulnerable to fluctuations in world markets). Bennett and his Cabinet responded by announcing an "economy with efficiency" drive; in other words, a drastic cutback in government spending. As education and welfare funding were cut back, and hundreds of government employees thrown out of work, a general disaffection with the regime began to emerge. As criticism of the government mounted, Bennett began to perceive conspiracies among the "special interests"—labour leaders, welfare professionals, academics, federalists and the press barons—all of whom were working to undermine his "little government."

Again, Bennett responded audaciously. In February, 1957, Lands and Forests Minister Ray Williston unveiled an agreement between the government and Swedish industrialist Axel Wenner-Gren to develop the enormous Rocky Mountain Trench area in the northern reaches of the province. The plan called for a kind of industrial Disneyland on a scale unimagined in human history. Williston's announcement was met by press and opposition with catcalls and laughter. Journalist Jack Scott flew over the area and immortalized the proposed mega-project in a phrase:

Alice in Wenner-Gren Land

Bennett and his Cabinet colleagues were dismayed by public reaction to the plan, which was derisory in nearly every quarter. A Victoria newspaper headline screamed: "Industrialist wins exclusive rights over one-tenth of British Columbia!" Journalists eagerly profiled Alex Wenner-Gren in the press; the Swedish magnate had been involved in Nazi munitions during the war, had once been a friend of Hermann Göring, and had been blacklisted by the Allies for trading with Axis powers. Furthermore, Wenner-Gren had made equally colossal development initiatives (each including the futuristic monorail) in Rhodesia and Mexico, neither of which had come to fruition. At the same time, bagman Einar Gunderson came under heavy fire, when his appointment to the board of the Wenner-Gren B.C. Development Company was announced. Over the last four years, Gunderson had accumulated directorships in a number of private companies and well as the P.G.E. Railway, the Highways and Bridges Authority, Black Ball Ferries and a major construction company. Bennett was quick to defend his crony from conflict of interest charges, but as he did so, any magic in the huge development proposal disappeared.

In spite of an opening ceremony staged for the (never-to-be-built) Wenner-Gren railway, The Rocky Mountain Trench development faded rapidly away. But by the fall of '57, a new proposal emerged from the old one, and Bennett returned to the press confer-

ence table with an announcement he called "the most momentous I have ever made": a plan to quite literally change the climate of the north by creating the largest man-made lake in the world. This was the Peace River hydro-electric power development: the largest earth-filled dam in the world, producing 5 million horsepower, and promising to resuscitate the economy of the whole province. "What this means to the future of such centres as Prince George," he gurgled excitedly:

> What it means in the opening up of a vast new world for the use and livelihood of our growing population, what it will do to weather conditions and transportation in the area affected is almost too stupendous a subject to consider!

The announcement of the Peace River project brought Bennett into direct conflict with the federal government, who for some years had been negotiating with the Americans for hydroelectric development of the Columbia River in the south of the province. Denouncing the negotiation of down-river rights as "pink teas," Bennett proposed to take direct action in the Peace to save the provincial economy; and at the same time to take a direct hand in the Columbia talks in order to save the southern interior.

A "Two River" policy became Bennett's catch phrase for the next decade; and it was perhaps as close to real policy as his Social Credit government would ever come. It opened another epoch of raw development in the province, remembered by historians as:

The DAM YEARS

As the '50s drew to a close, the Social Credit position on organized labour continued to clarify itself. In 1958, the Seafarers International Union struck the CPR ferry service between Vancouver Island and the mainland. Workers on the competing Black Ball line organized sympathetic work stoppages, and the water transportation system ground nearly to a halt at the height of the tourist season. Bennett intervened dramatically by proclaiming the Civil Defense Act, and took over operation of the Black Ball Line. A few months later, acting outside of the parliamentary arena, and using the Toll Highways authority as agent, he simply bought the ferry line outright, for $7.8 million.

WELCOME TO THE

1958 Gov't Workers Strike

Supreme Court Injunctions
and paranoid positions adopted

In the next legislative session, the Socreds brought in Bill 43, a comprehensive restrictive labour bill outlawing sympathy-strikes, boycotts and secondary picketing, and making unions liable for prosecution as legal entities. In March, 11,000 government workers walked off the job demanding a royal commission report on civil service bargaining rights (which were then non-existent). The government took a paranoid position, defining the protest as "a taking-over, a usurpation, of the functions of government by persons not elected or responsible to the public of the province." The strike ended within four hours, by Supreme Court injunction, and was followed by a bill prohibiting the picketing of government buildings.

Bill 43 drew a strong response from the CCF and labour leaders, who were characterized by the Socreds as gangsters, selfish bureaucrats and agitators. Eric Martin, erstwhile physical-education. instructor, attacked the CCF in a ringing non-sequitor.

W.A.C. Bennett had by now developed a preference for spectacular extraparliamentary action. In the summer of '59, after seven years in power, he invited the citizenry of British Columbia to attend a gala ...

Incineration of the Public Debt

On August 1st, 1959, armoured trucks unloaded $70 million worth of cancelled bonds onto a raft floating in Okanagan Lake outside Bennett's home town of Kelowna. After a day of beachside festivities, the Premier and his ebullient Cabinet climbed into a motor launch and sped out to the raft with its gasoline-soaked cargo. While thousands cheered from the beaches, Bennett loosed a flaming arrow at the doomed vessel. The arrow hit the raft and bounced harmlessly into the water; but within seconds a boatload of match-carrying RCMP officers moved in to apply fire by hand. Flame erupted, oily smoke boiled into the atmosphere: eventually all that remained of the net direct debt of the province sank to the bottom of Lake Okanagan.

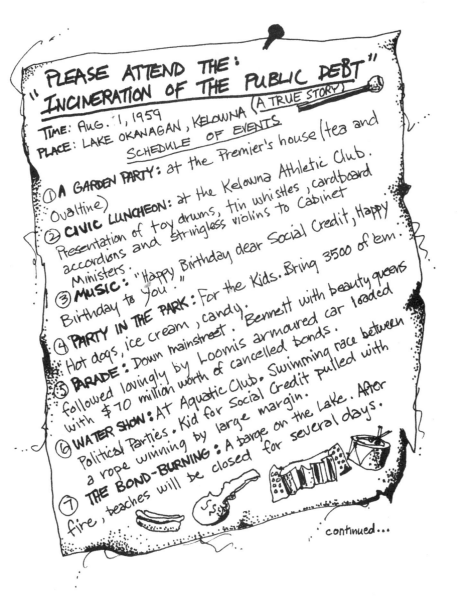

" PLEASE ATTEND THE:
INCINERATION OF THE PUBLIC DEBT"

TIME: AUG. 1, 1959 (A TRUE STORY)
PLACE: LAKE OKANAGAN, KELOWNA
SCHEDULE OF EVENTS

① A GARDEN PARTY: at the Premier's house (tea and Ovaltine)

② CIVIC LUNCHEON: at the Kelowna Athletic Club. Presentation of toy drums, tin whistles, cardboard accordions and stringless violins to Cabinet Ministers.

③ MUSIC: "Happy Birthday dear Social Credit, Happy Birthday to you."

④ PARTY IN THE PARK: For the Kids. Bring 3500 of 'em. Hot dogs, ice cream, candy.

⑤ PARADE: Down mainstreet. Bennett with beauty queens followed lovingly by Loomis armoured car loaded with $70 million worth of cancelled bonds.

⑥ WATER SHOW: At Aquatic Club. Swimming race between Political Parties. Kid for Social Credit pulled with a rope winning by large margin.

⑦ THE BOND-BURNING: A barge on the Lake. After fire, beaches will be closed for several days.

continued...

It was seven years to the day since the first Social Credit government in B.C. had been sworn in. "It took seventy years to build up the debt," Bennett revealed to his audience: "it took seven years to wipe it out!" Reminiscing for a friendly biographer in later years he would say, "I don't claim to be a Bible scholar, but this much I know: seven is an important number and cycles of seven appear throughout the Scriptures."

Not everyone agreed that a Seven Year Miracle had occurred: CCF leader Robert Strachan pointed out again and again that total provincial debt had in fact grown in that period from $195 million to $543 million; the Socreds had simply transferred liabilities from the government to Crown Corporations whose debts they continued to guarantee. Bennett had earlier forced the B.C. Power Commission to pay up a $30 million bond issue in order to clear the books; the Commission then had to reissue the bonds itself, at higher interest. Community newspapers throughout the province benefitted from fullpage government ads heralding the arrival of a debt-free Utopia.

In fact, B.C.'s total indebtedness in 1959, per capita, was the highest in Canada.

Bennett was by now a master of offensive politics. Rather than answer questioners from his legislative office, he took to the road: throughout 1959 and '60, he and his Cabinet journeyed through the province, "taking the government to the people." Cabinet meetings convened in nearly every city hall and municipal chambers in the province—receiving delegations from boards of trade, chambers of commerce, road-building associations, old age pensioners, farmers'

unions, mosquito control boards—and invariably concluded with announcements of new bridges, pieces of road, public buildings, community centres, or other tangibles. At one of these folksy meeting Bennett promised to annex the Yukon Territory, and extend B.C.'s northern border to the Beaufort Sea.

In preparation for an election in September 1960, Bennett finally announced a $10 billion ten-year highway construction program, an increase in homeowner's grants to $50.00, a $10 million increase in education spending, and a 20% increase in social welfare payments. For an election issue, he chose to do "battle to the death with big labour bosses."

The 1960 campaign proved to be the fiercest yet fought by B.C. Social Credit. The CCF, drawing unprecedented support from organized labour, ran an efficient campaign, well organized at the grass roots and clear in its definition of the issues. These were: public ownership of production and distribution of power, nationalization of B.C. Tel, Medicare, and the repeal of Bill 43.

The Socreds unleashed their rhetorical armament in an all-out attack on godless socialists. Presenting himself and his party as protectors of the "little man," Bennett defended private property and Bill 43 in a trembling voice:

> Because this little government had the nerve to put this Bill through, all these labour bosses are moving into B.C. in an invasion now ... If they had control of the government as well as the unions the men will have to jump every time these big labour bosses with their cigars and their hotel rooms snap their fingers.

Bennett's lieutenants joined him in a chorus of red-baiting, comparing Robert Strachan to Fidel Castro, and work conditions in socialist Saskatchewan to those in Soviet slave-labour camps. The Socreds were backed by smalltown newspapers in the Interior, who shared the perceived threat of "Marxian socialism"; and for the first time, big business interests actively aligned themselves with the populist party. The Vancouver Stock Exchange reminded voters that investors were "sensitive to nationalistic or socialistic attack"; the Federation of Trade and Industry, whose directors included the president of Peace River Power Development Company, the presidential assistant of B.C. Electric, and the vice-president of B.C. Tel, launched an advertising campaign illustrating the evils of socialism; and Frank McMahon, big boss of the Peace River oil and gas boom, president of Westcoast Transmission, implied in a public statement that a $450 million natural gas transmission line and 10,000 permanent jobs depended on re-election of the Socreds.

McMahon had good reason to support Bennett. His Westcoast Transmission Company owned the pipeline that supplied the American Northwest with natural gas from the Peace River Valley at bargain rates—a deal that might have created a few jobs, even though B.C. residents paid for it through gas rates one-third higher than the Americans paid for the same stuff.

The government barely survived the contest. In the closest election since 1952, the Socreds lost seven ridings and won 32, taking just over 38% of the vote. The CCF took 16 seats and 32% of the vote. The Liberal party took the remaining four seats.

The Socreds' clear majority masked the narrowness of the victory: a mere 4000 votes spread out over eight ridings had kept them in power.

Two Social Credit Cabinet ministers went down to defeat in 1960; one of them was Lyle Wicks, who lost to Dave Barrett, a young social worker who was fired when his employers at the Haney Correctional Institute learned he had won the CCF nomination.

The 1960 election served, however briefly, to chasten the Socreds, who were made by it to bleed a little. The ballot box had confirmed the very real presence of a palpable opposition not likely to disappear, while verifying that a reliable electoral bloc remained sympathetic to the rhetoric of paranoia and the style of strong-man populist politicking.

So, then, the '50s expired, as decades always do, but with the '50s ended also the period known among historians as ...

The SECULARIZATION of SOCIAL CREDIT

By the advent of the '60s, Social Credit in B.C. had shed the apocalyptic trappings of the Prophetic Bible Institute. Although P.A. Gaglardi kept up his public connection with the Man Upstairs, and Bennett himself would even claim (in a headline published in the Toronto *Globe*) to be "plugged into God," Social Credit rhetoric was by now generally couched in secular terms.

But in the 28 years since Social Credit first encroached upon Canadian political life, its rhetoric had really changed very little. Gone were the ogres of big business and "monopoly"; they were usurped now in the Social Credit nightmare by the ogres of organized labour and socialism (where they would be joined during the '60s by welfare recipients and the federal government).

The essential populist dream of the quick fix was still intact in old 1960, as it remains today: the Boom Without End and the Investment Climate might have replaced monetary reform in government policy, but the utopian nature of Socred rhetoric had not changed.

The monetary tinkerings proposed by Major Douglas, and promised by William Aberhart, had evolved under W.A.C. Bennett into the simple bookkeeping fictions familiar to any successful merchant: shift debt whenever necessary; use corporate fictions to keep the creditors from the door; use paper at all times. And remember, a moving target is hardest to hit.

Whereas William Aberhart had tried to run his government like a high school classroom, W.A.C. Bennett ran his like a hardware store.

WACKY, DEAR, IT'S A FRIEND OF HONEST BOB'S CALLING FROM SOME BACKWARD COUNTRY IN THE 3RD WORLD. WANTS YOUR OPINION ON WHETHER TO OPEN A HARDWARE STORE OR START A NEW GOVERNMENT...

WHAT'S THE DIFFERENCE? TELL HIM WHICH EVER HE DOES TO PUT THE EXPENSIVE MERCHANDISE WITH DISCOUNT PRICE TAGS IN THE WINDOW, SMILE EVERY MORNING AT THE EMPLOYEES AND KEEP THE DETAILS OF THE BUSINESS TO HIMSELF.

Welcome to A
Period of Legislation by Exhaustion
(Be prepared to spend many a night.)
Beware the Flying Fish!

JESUS, IT'S 4:00 AM! WON'T THEY EVER STOP?

B.C. PARLIAMENT BLDG.

Bennett ran a one-man government. His control over the Cabinet was total; all financial decisions rested with him. Bennett could stop all construction in the province with a phonecall, and just as easily start it up again. The traditional Social Credit distrust of parliamentary procedure remained intact. Legislative sessions were usually short and snappy. (Bennett referred to the sessions disdainfully as "talk, talk, talk.") But whenever the opposition tried to engage the government in debate, he would let the session continue on through the night, until everyone had run out of steam. As a parliamentary technique, this became known as "legislation by exhaustion." The real legislative power lay in orders-in-council issued by the Cabinet whenever Bennett felt it was time to take action. The real Social Credit forum was always the mass media.

But in the House, Bennett could be, in the words of Robert Strachan, "a pretty formidable character":

> It was very frightening at times, especially when he gave what we called his flying-fish act. He gave it about four times a session; he had it letter-perfect and word-perfect and gesture-perfect. The backbenchers knew all the cues and they would applaud and cheer and hurrah. He had all these phrases that just rolled off

and he was great ... He'd go on for about an hour and the place would be in an uproar. He would talk about the PGE railways as "the brightest jewel in our crown"; and "this little government" and he'd go right through their history about all that they'd done. He'd go on about the awful opposition throwing "sand in the gears." He'd have all the Socreds pounding their desks and their eyes would be sparkling and they'd be grinning from ear to ear. It was quite a show. He hadn't talked about the particular piece of legislation we were on, but that was all right—it wasn't great debate, but it was a good circus.

W.A.C. Bennett held onto power for twelve more years after the 1960 election. Supremely confident, he would say to a reporter in 1969: "My friend, I have no intention of retiring. Like a brook, I am going to go on and on forever."

W.A.C. Bennett held onto power for twelve more years after the 1960 election. Supremely confident, he would say to a reporter in 1969: "my friend, I have no intention of retiring. Like a brook, I am going to go on and on forever."

Secular Social Credit achieved its zenith in B.C. in the '60s: a period of tumult and untrammelled exploitation. W.A.C. Bennett provided the tumult; American, European and Japanese corporations provided the exploitation. At the heart of Bennett's vision lay, as ever, Wenner-Gren Land: Peace River country. As Bennett himself put it, exploiting the Peace meant:

La DOLCE VITA for all our PEOPLE

RECIPE for a BOOM

Let no one throw sand in the gears.
—W.A.C. Bennett

1. Get a stranglehold on the Federal government in Ottawa

2. Expropriate the BC Electric Company

3. Shake hands with John F. Kennedy

4. Get on the cover of Time Magazine (international edition)

5. Burn another barge filled with cancelled bonds

6. Oh yeah, start a national bank

7. Change the climate in the Peace River valley

8. Unleash the Social Credit Miracle Dividend Budget

9. Let the Dolce Vita ensue

Bennett had two figurative rivers to cross before he could start construction on the Peace: one in the form of the federal government, and the other in the privately-owned BC Electric Company. The federal government had been negotiating the development of the Columbia River system with the Americans for some years. The Columbia flows south over the border; the Americans wanted Canadian dams upstream to merely control the flooding of the river so that they could build power-generating dams downstream. The Canadians wanted to retain downstream control by generating power on the northern side, and selling it within B.C. and over the border.

BC Electric was the sole distributor of power throughout the province. It supported the Canadian proposal, because the power to be generated on the Canadian side would be cheaper than power from the Peace River. If the Canadian proposal were to go through, the Peace development, having lost its only potential market—BC Electric—would be scuttled.

Bennett supported the American proposal. He wanted to sell downstream rights to them for 30 years in return for a flat fee—that fee to be enough to pay for building three flood control dams on the Canadian side. His rationale was that the Columbia development would then be free to Canadians, who would eventually get free power from them. As he remarked in a characteristic aside:

This was the basis of the Bennett's Two River Policy. The Feds, who were worried about questions of sovereignty as well as economics, strongly resisted it, and refused to countenance the longterm alienation of downstream rights; B.C. Electric refused to cooperate in any way.

But W.A.C. Bennett was a man of bold action, and bold action is what he took. On July 31, 1961, as the CCF party began the convention that would transform it into the New Democratic Party, he convened a special session of the Legislature. The Lieutenant-Governor wound up the shortest throne speech on record with the announcement of "a Bill concerning the development of electric power resources."

Bill No. 5, as it came to be known, empowered the government to expropriate BC Electric, the largest privately-owned power company in Canada. It was a dramatic *coup de main*: the socialists in the CCF-NDP, for whom the take-over of BC Electric had been a central election plank, were dumbfounded. The world of big business panicked: *Barrons*, the leading American financial paper, under the headline "Lust for Power," compared Bennett's government to that of "a so-called People's Republic"; the *Financial Post*, somewhat incongruously, called Bennett "Moses on a Moutaintop." The expropriation made headlines all over the industrial world. In a comparison favoured by countless editorial writers, W.A.C. Bennett became the Fidel Castro of capitalism.

It's hard to say who might have been more offended, Bennett or Castro. In any event, the takeover was bloodless: a lengthy court case eventually ended in a generous settlement with BC Electric shareholders, who were paid off at a rate far above market value, and a new Crown Corporation took on the cost of the takeover, which increased the province's indirect debt by $700 million. The market for Peace River power was secure, and Bennett was free to lower industrial power rates as much as he liked.

The federal government was another matter. John Diefenbaker's Tories, opposed to the incorporation of Canadian resources into the American economic system, supported existing federal legislation forbidding longterm alienation of downstream rights. Bennett fulminated at length in public about obstructionist, socialistically-minded feds—over whom he would briefly gain a stranglehold at the end of the surprisingly ...

Long Arm of the Social Credit Movement

Over the years, Social Credit had not confined its activities to the provinces of Alberta and B.C. Since the '30s, an activist national party had been occasionally winning a few seats in the federal parliament, but until the '60s those seats were limited to Alberta. The national Social Credit party had become a refuge for the movement's die-hard Douglasites, monetary fetishists and conspiracy-theorists (the by-now-forgotten Rev. Hansell among them).

By 1960, with not a single representative in parliament, Social Credit was thought by many to have disappeared from the national

"AS FAR AS WE'RE CONCERNED, THEY CAN PUT ALL THOSE MONTREAL INTELLECTUALS INTO A MONKEY-CAGE + CHARGE ADMISSION."

The REAL CAOUETTE

JOSEPH DAVID REAL CAOUETTE was born in 1917 at Amos, Quebec. He was 21 years old and a travelling grocery salesman when he became a Social Credit devotee in 1939. In 1945, he ran successfully for a federal seat and became the only Quebec Socred in parliament, an outspoken advocate of a $20 national dividend, reduced sales tax, and restoration of the five-cent soft drink. An admirer of the economic policies of Hitler and Mussolini, Caouette held onto his seat for only one term, after which he ran unsuccessfully in federal elections for the next twelve years. In 1958, by then a prosperous car dealer in the town of Rouyn, Quebec, he founded the Ralliement des Creditistes with a membership of about 150. Emulating William Aberhart, who had learned to use radio in the '30s, he began to experiment with short broadcasts on the private TV stations which were springing up throughout rural Quebec. After a shaky start before the cameras, he adopted a fiery, hectoring style that quickly attracted a following large enough to get him and 25 supporters into the federal parliament in 1962.

Caouette soon broke away from the Alberta-dominated national party; and for about fifteen years national Social Credit existed in two organized forms: francophone and anglophone. By the early '80s both had disappeared from Parliament. The national movement sank into obscurity but continues to avoid oblivion; from time to time its survivors still emerge to denounce conspiracies or (more recently) to endorse the South African government.

scene. But in 1961, a car dealer named Réal Caouette began appearing on private TV stations throughout rural Quebec, haranguing his audience on the virtues of doctrinal Social Credit. In a style described by a journalist as "combination William Aberhart, Dale Carnegie and Juan Peron," the beak-nosed fanatic had an hypnotic effect on his viewers: staring straight into the camera, he would fulminate non-stop for fifteen minutes at a time, denouncing bankers, politicians, socialists and intellectuals—punctuating his delivery with nihilistic slogans: "You've got nothing to lose— vote Social Credit!" "Put those Montreal intellectuals into a monkey cage and charge admission!" Denizens of the depressed Quebec hinterland responded eagerly; when the national Social Credit organization convened before the federal election in 1962, Caouette had added 15,000 smalltown and rural Quebeckers to its membership roll.

Perceiving an opportunity to engage himself and his cause at the national level, W.A.C. Bennett took his Cabinet to the national Socred convention in Ottawa, where he threw his considerable weight behind the Roman Catholic firebrand. Ernest Manning, until now the *eminence grise* of the national organization, and afraid of losing Protestant support, resisted the Caouette leadership initiative by supporting his own candidate, a chiropractor named Robert Thompson. Thompson, an uncolourful figure, was noted for his mixed metaphors: "If this thing starts to snowball," he told the convention, "it will catch fire right across the country."

It was a stormy meeting, but Manning's candidate took the leadership by a close vote and quickly appointed Caouette deputy leader to avoid a francophone revolt. During the ensuing election campaign, W.A.C. Bennett and his dutiful Cabinet slogged through the backroads of Quebec, offering themselves in broken French as fleshy evidence of Social Credit at work. That work bore fruit: Social Credit sent 30 members to parliament, 26 of them from Quebec; enough to control the minority Tory government of John Diefenbaker.

W.A.C. Bennett emerged as the man with the pipeline to Réal Caouette, who forced the desperate Tories to reverse their protectionist stand on longterm export of power surpluses. The way was opened for Bennett to sell out the Columbia River development to the Americans, and the "Two River Policy" became a reality.

The B.C. resource boom peaked in the mid-60s when hardly a month went by without an announcement of another major industrial project. Pulp and paper mills, cement works, copper and molybdenum mines began opening up at a breath-taking pace. Companies from nearly every European nation, the U.S., Japan and Canada poured billions of dollars into resource extraction. Net value of forest products skyrocketed; the population began to rise rapidly, and a construction boom ensued as demand for city office space and residential housing increased. Short-term employment increased as profits earmarked for out-of-province investors took off.

1964: Vancouver. W.A.C. Bennett lobs flares onto a barge bearing $90 million worth of gasoline-soaked cancelled bonds. "Another little fire of progress in British Columbia," he called it. "Let no one throw sand in the gears."

1965: Portage Dam, Peace River. W.A.C. Bennett presses a button setting in motion a $10 million conveyor system geared to haul a million truckloads of gravel from a glacial moraine to the site the massive Portage Mountain Dam.

A month later, he changed the sign on his office door to read Prime Minister instead of Premier.

1965: Duncan Dam, Columbia River. After disembarking from a special train carrying a hundred personally invited guests, W.A.C. Bennett touches off 2 tons of dynamite, blowing a huge hole in the mountainside. The celebration is paid for by the Hydro Authority (sparing the government direct liability). After the explosion, Bennett hops a jet to Japan, where industrialists await him.

1967: 600 feet above the Peace River canyon. W.A.C. Bennett hops aboard a giant belly-dump Caterpillar to release the final 80 tons of fill into the W.A.C. Bennett Dam. Rarely–perhaps never–has a work of such monumentality been named after a living person. But the Lieutenant-Governor and local Peace River enthusiasts wanted it that way. The dam contains enough dirt to build a twelve-foot hill nine feet thick from Vancouver to Halifax. The enormous man-made slough that will collect behind it, filled with drowned forests, farms, and wildlife, will be called Williston Lake, named after his trusted Cabinet colleague. Gordon Shrum, wizening head of B.C. Hydro, compared Bennett to King Khufu, and the dam to the pyramid of Gizeh. Riposted Shrum: "The Pharoah went broke building the pyramid. We intend to make it pay."

Bennett modestly predicted that the dam bearing his name into posterity would "bring the greatest prosperity this province has ever known—LA DOLCE VITA for all our people."

1966: Free Enterprise at Work, Prince George. Ben Ginter, a local entrepreneur who would make $22 million in highway construction and pulp mills, prudently bought up large chunks of land surrounding Prince George before beginning construction of pulp mills along the river banks. "When those pulp mills start producing," he told an enchanted Time reporter, "that stench is going to sit right down there in the valley. And people are going to start scrambling up the hills to build their homes. And they're going to build them on my land."

The economic upsurge was hailed enthusiastically in the foreign press. The *Wall Street Journal* called it "Bennett's Boom"; and Bennett's career achieved its apogee when *Time* magazine graced the cover of its international edition with a foldout portrait of the pudgy Premier posing before a panorama of oil rigs, saw mills, power dams, totem poles and harbourfront. "It's extremely flattering for a humble little chap from New Brunswick to get in *Time*," he told reporters, "not only in Canadian and U.S. editions, but world editions as well. This will bring tremendous results. It will get millions and millions of new investment and new industries and its all bound to be on the plus side."

Social Credit was entering into an epoch of state capitalism. Under W.A.C. Bennett, British Columbia had come to resemble an independent capitalist state: an activist, interventionist government acting as a full partner in the corporate assault on the frontier. It was a state with its own railway, a navy (in the form of the ferry system), an airforce (eight planes owned by the Highways Department), a public power authority engaged in a project the size of the Aswan Dam in Egypt, and a provincial bank. (The bank, part of Bennett's plan to "help every little capitalist," would take another year or so before emerging as the somewhat unstable Bank of British Columbia—not to be confused with Major Douglas's National Credit Authority.)

The Socreds won the election of '63, to the tune of brass bands playing "Roll On, Social Credit, Roll On," on a platform combining opposition to the federal government, which had become, in the panoply of Social Credit ogres, an obstructionist force tainted with leftist corruption, and the usual anti-socialist rhetoric. A beaming P.A. Gaglardi said to his constituents on victory night, "Tomorrow morning I'll head for my office and let a whole bunch more highway contracts." In 1966 Bennett went to the people again, this time demanding the complete defeat of his parliamentary Opposition, who, he claimed, represented "chaos" as opposed to the "stability" a one-party government could be expected to maintain. This bid for supreme power went unheeded by 54% of the population, but the remaining 46% were enough to keep his government in with a slightly reduced majority.

The Social Credit heydey was marred briefly when Opposition members charged in the House that P.A. Gaglardi's sons were getting rich buying up land along proposed highway routes, and selling it to oil companies eager to erect gas stations. On top of that, he had engaged the Highways Department to work for nothing on his ranch; supported land re-zoning applications made by his sons; and had flown his daughter-in-law, among others, to Texas in a Department jet.

Gaglardi's emotional response brought tears to the eyes of W.A.C. Bennett. The embattled Pentecostal claimed the charges were the result of a sinister gangland plot to embarass him and destroy the government:

After a tepid inquiry, Gagliardi resigned from the Cabinet, but kept his seat. While defending his sons, he inadvertently summed up the free enterprise ethical position:

> Just because their father was Highways Minister, did that mean these boys had to be second-class citizens ... Weren't they entitled to do what any other private citizen could do?

The 1969 election returned Social Credit with its largest majority ever, prompting Bennett to announce that the Socreds "had saved Canada from socialism."

Social Credit entered the '70s complacently, continuing to dispense tangibles to grateful voters, while keeping the door open for corporate frontiersmen. But even as Bennett's adpeople were announcing that the Good Life had descended upon the citizenry (in an execrable movie of that name), the worm, so to speak, had already begun to eat the apple. In two short years, Bennett's dream of the Endless Boom would evaporate, his party would be in shreds and his career as boss politician at an end, in a brief period felt by many to be a kind of latterday...

GOTTERDAMMERUNG...

Pulp mills and saw mills began closing down at an alarming rate. Strikes and lockouts proliferated; Columbia River megaprojects came to a close, throwing hundreds out of work. Within a year, welfare rolls increased by nearly 50%. Bennett tried to solve the growing jobless problem by renaming the Welfare Department the "Department of Social Improvement, Rehabilitation and Human Resources."

AND PUT THE DISTINGUISHED PHIL GAGLARDI BACK IN ACTION BY MAKING HIM *WELFARE MINISTER* TO - AS HE PUT IT - "*WEED OUT THE DEADBEATS*"...

BELIEVE ME, I'M GONNA BE " THE ROUGHEST, TOUGHEST, MOST EFFECTIVE WELFARE MINISTER THE WORLD HAS EVER KNOWN!"

AND FINALLY, GET THE **W.A.C.** OUT THERE TO BLAME SOMEONE FOR IT ALL, AS DOCTORS, TEACHERS, STUDENTS AND THE POP. IN GENERAL START TO EXPRESS THEIR *CHAGRIN* ABOUT THE ECONOMIC *MALAISE* ...

"HERE IS THIS LITTLE SOCIAL CREDIT GOVERNMENT TRYING TO FIND JOBS AND THESE **LABOUR BOSSES** KNOCK IT AND TRY TO KEEP PEOPLE ON WELFARE. I DON'T KNOW WHERE THEIR HEART OR SOUL IS."

HELP?

AND SO...

THE GOOD LIFE

More and more people were discovering that the Good Life was postulated on an economy that couldn't deliver; an economy skewed toward the capital intensive resource sector, employing proportionally fewer and fewer people as profits increased; an economy that sucked profits out of the province, while creating almost no permanent jobs within the province. The economy of the Good Life presumed an ever-expanding market, an ever-expanding foreign investment base, and a never ending supply of raw materials. None of these conditions prevailed in 1972, nor have they since.

Like Social Credit in Alberta, B.C. Social Credit had presumed too much. Foreign capital, given free access to resources and an infrastructure paid for by taxpayers, comes and goes as world markets dictate, taking profit where it can. When it leaves, it leaves behind it a wasteland.

Thousands of square miles of devastated, unreforested timber land, excavated mountainsides and polluted waterways were all that remained of the profit-taking epoch.

Generally, it was an evil time for Social Credit. The Legislative Building in Victoria was stormed by disgruntled students, and again by disaffected farmers. Nowhere in the evolved Social Credit analysis of the world was there a rhetoric broad enough to embrace what seemed to be happening: enemies of the regime cropping up in every quarter.

In the spring of 1972, an embattled W.A.C. Bennett, recalling his roots among those he called "the people," packed up his Cabinet and set out on a 3000-mile good-will tour of the province—a journey that would make its way into legend as ...

The tour was a disaster. Unruly crowds appeared everywhere along the route; in New Westminster they attacked and were beaten back by police. Finally, a disenchanted W.A.C. Bennett resolved to meet the dissidents head on in an electoral fight to the finish. "I want to tell you tonight," he thundered at a party rally ...

"The SOCIALIST HORDES are at the GATES!"

On August 30, 1972, Social Credit went down to a resounding defeat, hanging on to a mere ten seats. The NDP, under ex-social worker Dave Barrett, took 38, the Liberals five and the Conservatives two. Only a year after the collapse of Social Credit in Alberta, the B.C. movement had fallen apart in a rout unforeseen by a single political commentator. In the hushed silence that followed, it looked like Social Credit had run itself into the ground. Tories and Liberals began covetously to dream of forming the Opposition, while the NDP eagerly took their seats on the government side of the House to commence a program that would introduce more major pieces of legislation in three years than their predecessors had in ten.

The NDP had to work fast, of course, because three years was all the time they had. For while they were busy setting up Community Resouce Boards, bringing in public car insurance, creating Crown Corporations to revive dying industry, awarding collective bargaining rights to government employees—in short, enacting policy—a murky form was evolving out of the sands of the desert: a rough beast, its gaze blank and pitiless as the sun, its hour come round so soon, had begun to slouch towards Victoria to be born as ...

SON of SOCRED

During the latter years of W.A.C. Bennett's sovereignty, the B.C. Social Credit League had been left to fester; by 1972, its membership had dwindled to some 4000 hardcore Socreds. A University of Victoria study of party delegates in 1973 offered this analysis of their backgrounds: slightly more than a fifth of party activists were small proprietors, managers and officials; another fifth were housewives; 16% were clerks and salespeople; 13% were professionals, and 3% were big businessmen. Nearly a quarter of them earned more than $20,000 a year (as opposed to a mere 7% of the NDP); only a third had any university education, but more than 90% professed the Christian religion.

In 1973 this hardy band of free-enterprisers met to breathe new life into Social Credit by electing as their party leader a man with no political experience but plenty of the right kind of connections: W.A.C. Bennett's land-developing son, Bill, whose destiny it would be to drag Social Credit into the steaming '80s.

The younger Bennett, lacking even the flying-fish charisma of his father, was a dull man with a wooden manner; but for his illustrious bloodlines, he seemed at first glance to be an unlikely

---

The history of Bill Bennett's time in office has been well chronicled in two entertaining books by Stan Persky: *Son of Socred* and *Bennett II.* Highly recommended.

choice for the floundering Socreds. In two short years, however, he would prove himself equal to the challenge.

WHO?

WILLIAM RICHARDS BENNETT was born in Kelowna, B.C, 14 April, 1932, the child of W.A.C. and May Bennett. As a millionaire's son, he delivered newspapers, worked in a plumbing shop, and then bought his first commercial building (with brother R.J.) before finishing highschool. Although Bill claims to have had an ambition to go to university and become a lawyer, his highschool annual prognosticated more accurately that he "would work, as little as possible, in the local branch of Bennett's Stores."

A merchant at 18 with good connections has nowhere to go but up, and up is where young Bill went. At 23 he married Audrey Jones, a nurse's aid at the Kelowna General, and rapidly ensconced her in a lakeside ranch house with garburetor. She has continued to be his wife ever since. The adventurous couple were soon forced to sell the ranch house, in order to buy into a motel with Bill's sister. Then, fighting hard times, the feisty entrepreneur got involved (inevitably) in renovating run-down office buildings. He bought a ranch, a saw mill, a finance company, and some pieces of real estate on the hill overlooking the river. Hedging against inflation, young Bill found himself with no choice but to participate in a $34 million shopping mall, along with the irrepressible R.J and some childhood friends in the Capozzi family.

Sooner or later, Bill Bennett would become the top politician in B.C., and Audrey would have to drive all the way to the Kelowna airport in a snowstorm, just to get Bill's tuxedo down to Victoria in time for some fancy dinner.

When the NDP government chose, for reasons unknown to history, to call an early election in the fall of '75, Bill Bennett was ready with a powerful electoral machine backed by an enormous slush fund and powerful corporate partisans. Private insurance companies ran a media scare campaign of their own; mining and timber barons made political speeches; and Bill Bennett promised a return of "good government," in a campaign directed at middle-of-the-road voters, who were warned endlessly of the dire consequences of vote-splitting. (In the '72 election, 30% of the vote had gone to fringe Liberal and Conservative candidates.)

The campaign proved successful as erstwhile Liberal and Tory voters crossed the line in thousands. On Dec 11th, 1975, a date consecrate by pundits as "the Night of the Car Dealers," Social Credit returned to the halls of government, transfused by new blood, and eager to begin remaking history.

Like his father, Bill Bennett was not a bookish man. As a political thinker he had little to offer the student of political process; statements about government and politics he couched in incomprehensible homilies riddled with free enterprise jargon. As a political leader, he would have to earn his niche in Social Credit history by his actions alone.

In his first political act, the appointment of a Cabinet, Bill Bennett, perhaps unwittingly, established the ethical framework within which Social Credit would go forward into the inflationary times ahead of it. The new Human Resources Minister, a renegade Liberal named Bill Vander Zalm, was the first of Bennett's lieutenants to begin the random policy-making procedure that would become a hallmark of his government's style. Vander Zalm welcomed his Cabinet appointment at a champagne dinner by promising to track down the welfare deadbeats that P.A. Gaglardi had been unable to find, and to hire as many welfare police as might be needed to do it. As for the poor who were not maimed, crippled or otherwise handicapped, he promised to give them shovels; if any were to refuse such aid, he warned, "we will find ways of dealing with him!"

Tom Waterland, on the other hand, as the new non-Human Resources Minister, took another tack. To ease the plight of his corporate wards, he promised to repeal NDP mining legislation, and to eliminate mining royalties completely.

WELCOME TO THE "CONSUMER AFFAIRS MINISTER'S" THOUGHTS ON CONSUMER PROTECTION IN THE FREE-ENTERPRISE SYSTEM:

"I THINK ONE OF THE CHARACTER BUILDERS OF THIS WORLD IS TO ALLOW PEOPLE TO TAKE THE INITIATIVE AND GET KICKED IN THE ASS UNTIL THEY FINALLY LEARN TO TAKE THEIR LUMPS!"

RAFE MAIR

WELCOME TO A WARNING FROM THE "HEALTH MINISTER":

HEY, VICTORIA, AND OTHER B.C. CITIES! BE ON THE LOOKOUT FOR NON-EXISTENT DRUG AND PROSTITUTION RINGS!

IN 1985 I MYSELF WILL BE IMPLICATED IN A SLEAZY BAWDY HOUSE TRIAL IN VICTORIA.

BOB McCLELLAND

WELCOME TO THE "PROVINCIAL SECRETARY" AND "MINISTER OF TOURISM"...

I IMMEDIATELY CUT BUDGET FUNDING FOR THE "B.C. STATUS OF WOMEN" BELIEVING THAT ORGANIZED WOMEN JUST AREN'T NATURAL (and I should know being quite unnatural myself)— AT THE SAME TIME BILLY [VANDER ZALM] HELPED OUT BY ELIMINATING 4 TRANSITION HOUSES FOR BATTERED WOMEN!

SIGH!

GRACE McCARTHY

"OUR LADY OF OIL OF OLAY"

WELCOME TO AN EDUCATION FROM THE "EDUCATION MINISTER":

"IF YOU CAN'T AFFORD INSURANCE FOR IT [YOUR CAR], SELL IT!"

BELIEVE IT OR NOT, I WAS A BRAIN RESEARCHER BEFORE TAKING OFFICE, BUT REFUSED ANY WORK IN THIS FIELD TO BE DONE ON MYSELF OR ANY OTHER MEMBER IN THE PARTY. I ALSO TOOK CHARGE OF THE "ICBC" (a newly formed public car insurance corporation) AND PREMIUMS SKYROCKETED!

PAT McGEER

214

The younger Bennett's father had helped shape the myth of the corporate frontiersmen by aligning himself with their assault on the non-sentient resources of the province. Trees without voices, dumb rocks, inarticulate rivers and lakes, whispering fish: these were the objects of W.A.C. Bennett's passion during the time of the Endless Boom.

Times had changed by 1975; from the day he took office, Bill Bennett directed his assault against the *human* resouces of the province, as Social Credit, its own intellectual resources by now pretty well exhausted, moved into the Time of ...

The New Brutalism

Social Credit returned to power in B.C. without a single policy initiative; its sole motive ground seems to have been a superstitious belief that the NDP interregnum had stained the virtue of the people, who must be made to pay for it. Early in his first term, a deadpan Bill Bennett announced to the world that his precedessors had "lost" half a billion dollars, which would have to be recovered by stringent measures.

The loss, it turned out, was a paper loss created by the Socreds themselves fiddling the books. Even Bennett's bookkeepers couldn't justify it. But this didn't stop Evan Wolfe from increasing sales and personal income tax, hospital and medicare fees by $267 million, while repealing mining royalties.

Pat McGeer tried to set the stage for dismantling the public insurance corporation (the ICBC, an NDP initiative) by jacking up rates astronomically; Transport Minister Jack Davis followed suit by doubling ferry rates; Vander Zalm widened his campaign to include the destruction of the NDP's Community Resources Board—a moderate experiment in local decision-making that (briefly) involved municipalities in handling the welfare problem.

McGeer was forced to drop his plans for killing ICBC when 10,000 angry motorists rallied in protest; the increase in ferry rates resulted in a 30% decrease in ferry use, and a $5 million loss in tourist revenues on Vancouver Island.

In his first year, Vander Zalm's welfare crackdown netted him 67 deadbeats whose offenses averaged $910 each—apparently a high enough kill rate to justify a further expenditure of $720,000 in investigation and "rehabilitation." While unemployment hovered around the 10% mark, Vander Zalm announced a dress code for the poor, cut senior citizens with more than a miserable $2500 in assets off Mincome, cut payments to hundreds of handicapped people as a disincentive to potential deadbeats, threatened to cut off welfare recipients living in remote areas, and then threatened to proclaim Vancouver a welfare-free zone. He was a busy man, and perhaps the first welfare minister in history to turn a "profit": he underspent his budget by $100 million.

Grace McCarthy set out to save the recently wounded tourist industry by resurrecting the effigy of James Cook, a syphilitic sea captain who got lost in the fog off Vancouver Island two hundred years ago. (He was rescued by the Mowachaht people, whose descendants still sing unflattering songs about him.)

Bill Bennett managed to stay invisible while his Cabinet Ministers made fools of themselves. But a flurry of scandals drew him out of the woodwork briefly to order a judicial inquiry into a pipeline ripoff, a royal commission to look into BC Rail (the old PGE—whose screwy finances had finally come to light), and a house "investigation" into charges of civil servant blacklisting. In the same six-month period he was forced to issue a stern memo warning party members not to put close relatives into lucrative jobs; and to fire his transport Minister, Jack Davis, who was guilty of fraud.

It was a time of bumbling and incompetence. Labour Minister Alan Williams had to eat his own legislation, which was so incomprehensibly drafted no one could make sense of it; Agriculture Minister Jim Hewitt beat a swift retreat from his attempt to scrap the farmers assurance program when angry tractors began to appear on the highways.

By 1979, Social Credit seemed to have lost its utopian flavour: rudderless, it was no longer embedded in a *scheme*. Unemployment and inflation were at record levels; the spectre of welfare deadbeats loomed on the horizon—when Bill Bennett crawled back out of the woodwork to announce the dawning of yet another epoch in the evolution of Social Credit:

PEOPLE's CAPITALISM!

"ONLY USED CAR DEALERS CAN FIGURE OUT A WAY TO SELL YOU SOMETHING YOU ALREADY OWN." - NDP Leader, Dave Barrett

I'VE BEEN TOLD THAT DURING OUR, UH, "VACATION", THE *NDP* PURCHASED IN THE NAME OF THE PEOPLE A NUMBER OF RESOURCE-BASED HOLDINGS, MOSTLY IN THE FOREST INDUSTRY, AND THAT THESE VENTURES HAVE PROVEN SUCCESSFUL, UH, TURNING A TIDY PROFIT WHILE RETAINING JOBS... BUT, PUBLICLY-OWNED INDUSTRY, PROFITABLE OR NOT, HAS ALWAYS BEEN A... A...

ANATHEMA!

ANATHEMA TO OUR FREE-ENTERPRISE SYSTEM OF SOCIAL CREDIT!

SO WE BETTER COME UP WITH SOMETHING TO RELIEVE THE GOVERNMENT OF THIS, UH, THIS...

SOCIALIST BURDEN!

SOCIALIST BURDEN!

SON OF SOCRED

BCRIC

It was to be the last of the great Social Credit initiatives: a huge private corporation in which all of the citizenry would be shareholders: the BC Resources Investment Corporation (BCRIC, pronounced "brick").

By transferring publicly-owned holdings, as well as government petroleum and gas leases, licenses and permits, over to the new BCRIC, Bennett would be relieving the government of a socialist burden. At the same time, by allowing the public to invest in the new company, money hoarded away in savings accounts would be drawn into the investment economy, which would thereby be stimulated into creating new industry and new jobs.

In preparation for the 1979 election, Bill Bennett announced that five free shares in BCRIC would be issued to every man, woman and child in the province. "This is the commitment of our government to individual ownership rather than socialism or government ownership," he told voters: everyone would own "a piece of the rock." Furthermore, savings-hoarders could put their dollars to work by buying up to 5000 additional shares at $6.00 each.

The election came and went; Social Credit won by five seats. When the ensuing share-grabbing frenzy was over, 2 million B.C. citizens held ten million free shares, and 120,000 of them had thrown another $450 million into the BCRIC kitty, to create overnight a corporate giant. BCRIC president David Helliwell, a Bennett appointee, was thrilled. "It just sends shivers up my spine," he announced.

BCRIC shares went onto the stock exchange at $6.12 and B.C.'s neophyte capitalists began learning how to read stock quotations in the daily press. Most of them were still grappling with the fine print when BCRIC shares shot up to $9.00 on the strength of rumours that Prime Minister Joe Clark might sell it holdings owned by Petrocan, Canada's national oil company. A few experienced investors quickly took their profits and ran; within a month the stock was back to $6.00. For a year, nothing happened.

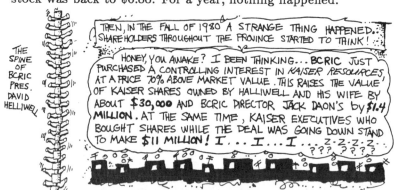

THE SPINE OF BCRIC PRES. DAVID HELLIWELL

THEN, IN THE FALL OF 1980 A STRANGE THING HAPPENED. SHAREHOLDERS THROUGHOUT THE PROVINCE STARTED TO THINK!

HONEY, YOU AWAKE? I BEEN THINKING... BCRIC JUST PURCHASED A CONTROLLING INTEREST IN KAISER RESOURCES AT A PRICE 70% ABOVE MARKET VALUE. THIS RAISES THE VALUE OF KAISER SHARES OWNED BY HALLIWELL AND HIS WIFE BY ABOUT $30,000 AND BCRIC DIRECTOR JACK DAON'S by $1.4 MILLION. AT THE SAME TIME, KAISER EXECUTIVES WHO BOUGHT SHARES WHILE THE DEAL WAS GOING DOWN STAND TO MAKE $11 MILLION! I... I... I... Z-Z-Z-Z ???.????

The Kaiser deal was followed by an abortive attempt to take over forest giant MacMillan Bloedel, and it became clear that BCRIC would have nothing to do with "stimulating" industry; nor would it create jobs for anyone other than its board of directors and their staff. A crowd of disgruntled shareholders learned at the 1981 annual meeting that even those few jobs were out of their control when they tried to unseat millionaires Jim Pattison and Chunky Woodward from the executive; not only were these luminaries re-seated, but they were joined by Edgar Kaiser and Jack Poole, along with others of their ilk.

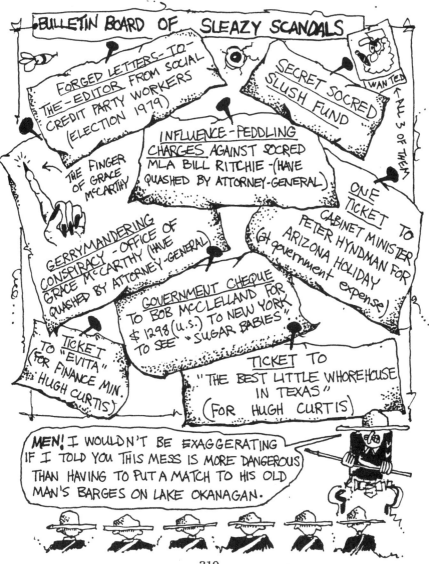

BCRIC shares have since maintained a downward climb on the exchange. Today they're worth about $1.30. B.C.'s citizen-investors are wiser now, and poorer by about $360 million.

Bill Bennett, who, a year after creating BCRIC, claimed proudly that the infant corporate giant "will always be in my mind," would later tell the press, "I don't know anything about it. It's a private sector company."

While the BCRIC fiasco ground on into the '80s, and a number of sleazy scandals came to light, new levels of cynicism began to emerge in the upper echelons of Social Credit. During this disagreeable time, the Social Credit party duly established an ethics committee—an unnecessary and redundant move, according to party president Whistling Bernie Smith, who argued that "this party doesn't need a code of ethics—it's built on Christian principles." Bill Bennett, whose disappearing act had become chronic in times of unpleasantness, decided to improve the government's soiled image by bringing in Los Angeles movie specialists to clean up his on-camera appearance.

BC Place: A giant pneumatic stadium in the middle of Vancouver that sprang from a $60 million land deal with Marathon Realty and culminated in the '86 World's Fair (Expo). It remains to be seen what benefits may accrue from this edifice, and future development of the surrounding land. Its construction, and the construction of the world's fair, sucked up millions of dollars from health and educational funds transferred from the federal to the provincial government—a price the Socreds maintain was worth it.

Northeast Coal: a project bigger than anything in provincial history, involving billions of dollars, a town, a port, and the opening of a vast investment frontier yet untouched by corporate marauders. Customer for the coal: the Japanese steel industry. Estimated loss on the project over the next 15 to 20 years: $500 million to $1 billion. It would have been cheaper to let the Japanese just come over and take the coal for free. Summed up by NDP analyst Stu Leggatt: "Japan gets the coal and we get the hole."

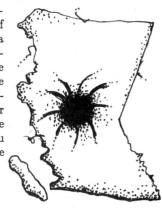

The full weight of the general recession hit B.C. in 1982; Social Credit, born politically in the Depression of the '30s, would prove sadly unequal to the challenge of depression in the '80s. While befuddled Finance Minister Hugh Curtis meditated semantic mysteries in public ("I have some difficulty determining what is a recession and what is a downturn"), Bill Bennett took to mumbling uncertainties about a concept he called "restraint"—a quantity that would remain undefined, although some of its qualities quickly made themselves manifest. As unemployment reached Depression levels, Social Credit made plans to throw thousands of government employees, school workers and teachers out of work. As foodbanks were springing up in church basements, new Human Resources Minister Grace McCarthy began cutting back payments to single parents, and disentitling old people to Pharmacare benefits.

Bill Vander Zalm led the assault on education. He justified the massive budget cuts by scapegoating educators and staff, whom he accused of being wasteful, overpaid, and incompetent. In order to "get back to the basics"—another undefined quantity—he even offered to write school curriculum himself.

Bennett's solution to the recession could be summed up in a phrase: more unemployment and wage cuts. When asked how he could justify increasing MLAs' salaries (many MLAs being millionaires) while cutting back on workers' wages, Bennett offered this insight: "I guess out there there are a lot of workers who are millionaires who also work."

Public protest was enormous. Bennett and his ministers backtracked, sidestepped, and strove for high seriousness. In 1983, preparing for another election, Bennett softened his rhetoric and began to meditate publicly about "recovery," while focussing public attention on the Expo megaproject. The rhetorical combination of restraint, recovery and glitz worked— to the surprise of just about everyone including the Socreds, who were returned to power on a platform that seemed to imply that they would "take it easy on restraint."

By 1983, food banks had begun to proliferate all over the province. As unemployment soared, the destitute were lining up in increasing numbers: a living emblem of Aberhart's old battle cry:

Poverty in the Midst of Plenty!

Over the next three years Bill Bennett displayed all the symptoms of a man searching desperately for truth. He began by calling in experts from the Fraser Institute, a right-wing thinktank once regarded as part of the lunatic fringe of Canadian politics. The meet-

ing resulted in the now-infamous budget of 1983, and a legislative package unprecedented in Canadian history.

In an scattergun assault on all but the non-corporate sectors of society, Bennett and his lieutenants introduced 26 new bills that would, among other things:

— repeal the Human Rights Code and abolish the Human Rights Commission;
— abolish rent controls;
— remove non-residential taxing authority from school boards, and put school board budgets under ministerial control;
— eliminate local representation on college boards, while establishing ministerial control over courses and budgets; eventually, grants to students would be eliminated too;
— eliminate motor vehicle testing;
— wipe out municipal regional planning;
— wipe out minimum employment standards (safety, pregnancy, etc) from all collective agreements;
— cut spending in health, education and welfare;
— eliminate government workers rights' to negotiate job security, working conditions, transfers, etc;

The resulting outcry surprised the optimistic Socreds, who were moved to physically haul NDP leader Dave Barrett out of the House and forbid him re-entry; photographers as well were banned from the corridors of Parliament.

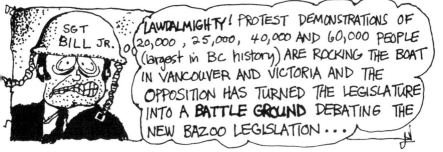

Bennett strove for complacency throughout the storms of '83–'84. As an alternative to answering embarassing questions from Opposition or journalists, he hired public opinion experts as advisors, and began paying close attention to their polls as indicators of the correctness of his actions. Pesky media people he sought to avoid by constructing an inner staircase running from his office into another, to allow him a secret exit (billed as a fire escape for budgetary purposes—possibly the only fire escape in the world leading from one closed room to another).

By early summer of 1986, even with Expo pulling in 120,000 people a day, the opinion polls were still bleak, and Bill Bennett's chances in another election were at an all-time low. Rather than face the likelihood of an electoral Waterloo, he decided abruptly to get out of political life altogether. No one in his own party, the media or the public was prepared when he announced his immediate retirement from public life.

"I quit," said the Premier, and the Bennett dynasty was no more.

GHOST of SOCRED

"I AM NOT ABOUT TO CHANGE MY STYLE AFTER 18 YEARS."
—1982

The FANTASY PREMIER

WILHELMUS NICHOLAAS THEODORE MARIA VANDER ZALM is the son of a Dutch tulip bulb salesman. He followed his father into the bulb business, and at 21 opened a garden centre of his own which would eventually grow into a chain of nurseries. In 1965 he ran successfully as alderman in the Vancouver suburb of Surrey; three years later he became mayor and discovered a passion for searching out welfare deadbeats—whose depredations were apparently undermining the economy and the quality of Surrey life. This passion he was able to carry into provincial politics when Bill Bennett invited him into a revamped Social Credit party in 1975. As a Cabinet Minister, Vander Zalm quickly developed a notoriety for shooting from the lip; his ugly jokes about Francophone Canadians, for example, earned him headlines across the country. Perceived by his partisans to be a man unafraid to speak his mind, Vander Zalm has advocated castration for heroin dealers, grooming standards for welfare recipients, and suspension of welfare payments in regions where hallucinogenic mushrooms grow wild.

An opponent of decentralization and local democracy, Vander Zalm fought hard to destroy Community Resources Boards and to undermine the autonomy of school and college boards. He is a devout anti-abortionist and opposes the feminist movement—although he claims to be able to appreciate women because they have "more ESP" than men (his wife Lillian has endorsed this insight.)

Vander Zalm left politics in 1983 to devote himself to the cultivation of Fantasy Gardens, a kind of floral Disney Land, where he resides today with his wife and well-scrubbed family— all of whom seem to possess perfect teeth. In 1986 he took up the leadership of the ailing Social Credit Party. He won the '86 election handily with no platform and a vague promise to lower the price of beer. A handsome and personable man, Vander Zalm exercises a charismatic hold over his many followers (but not his mother-in-law, who continues to support the NDP).

Bill Bennett's political exit was abrupt: historically speaking, he was there one minute and gone the next.

A dozen eager Socreds rushed into the ensuing vacuum to offer themselves in Bennett's place at a song-and-balloon leadership convention in the resort town of Whistler Mountain. Candidates fell into two camps: establishment figures associated with the old regime, and anti-establishment figures like Grace McCarthy and Bill Vander Zalm.

Vander Zalm had come into the race as the dark horse. Three years earlier, at the time of the '83 election, he had dropped out of provincial politics, apparently disgusted with Cabinet colleagues who refused to support a land-use bill that would have wiped out municipal control over zoning and land development. By the time of his retirement, Vander Zalm had become the most combative and confrontational of Bennett's lieutenants, having wreaked havoc in welfare, education and municipal affairs, and left Bennett reeling in the wash of public protest.

At the 1986 Social Credit leadership convention, Bill Vander Zalm presented himself as a changed man, speaking confidently in tones of moderation and accommodation. Without accusing anyone directly, he implied that the old regime had drifted too far into confrontational attitudes, and that he, in his non-confrontational mode, was the man to lead Social Credit out of the desert into which Bill Bennett had lured it. In three years, he had achieved a remarkable transformation. Once the *bête noire* of confrontational politics, he seemed to embody the possibility of change for Social Credit: the kind of fresh start that all the candidates were promising, but only he could present in his own flesh.

As the ballotting proceeded, more and more delegates went over to the Vander Zalm camp—charmed by the handsome, smiling handshaker who uttered only harmless platitudes. Grace McCarthy made a last ditch plea for attention by promising to cut off *all* welfare recipients in order to make a fresh start, but fewer and fewer delegates were listening to her, or to any of the crowd of upstaged candidates. When the ballotting was over, and balloons were popping flatulently all over the hall, Bill Vander Zalm, new champion of moderation and the "little guy," was the leader of the Social Credit movement.

In 1935, William Aberhart had gone to the people with the simple request that they take him and Social Credit on faith or not at all; in 1986, William Vander Zalm went to the people with the same request. He cakewalked through the campaign, shaking hands and kissing babies. "Let me worry about things for a while," he seemed to be saying, "you take it easy."

At a rally in Smithers, a young woman asked him to explain the Social Credit position on Education, Health and Welfare, permanent jobs, and trade unions. Vander Zalm's reply was forthright, to say the least: "Well, if you want those things, then you should vote NDP." The crowd of Smithers citizens responded with laughter and applause.

Half the voters in the province laughed too: Vander Zalm brought the Socreds out of the slough of despond and back into office with a smile and a handshake.

Vander Zalm was careful throughout the campaign, as he has been since the election, to avoid the traditional Socred rhetoric of scapegoating and red-baiting. Questioned about his position on the infamous food banks that are now a feature of B.C. life (and Bill Bennett's only real legacy), he retreats from direct statement with dark hints that the food banks (in Socred eyes possibly a good thing because they represent "individual enterprise"), are of course breeding grounds for freeloaders—the deadbeats in vain pursuit of whom he and Phil Gaglardi have spent millions of taxpayers' dollars—a reminder that somewhere among us continues to lurk the spectre of the undeserving poor.

By 1986 the Social Credit tradition of conspiracy theories, racism and crackpot economics seemed to have devolved upon the national Social Credit Party, which still clings to organizational life, if refusing to concede political death. Its 1986 convention generated a resolution in support of the white South African government; present as an "observer" was Ernst Zundel, a convicted hate-mongerer whose anti-semitic pro-Hitler publications sparked a trial making Canada the only country in the world to feel obliged to prove in court that the Holocaust really happened.

Meetings of the national Social Credit organization are routinely graced by speakers eager to illuminate the intricate workings of the mythical Conspiracy to Enslave Us All: the unlikely and frightening combination of Bankers and Communists, and of course, the Jews. In 1984, the national Socred vice- president warned the world yet again of the "Zionist conspiracy,"—"a plan by those people to establish a one-world dictatorship." Among his audience was the chameleon-like William Vander Zalm, special guest speaker.

Vander Zalm, queried on the tradition of anti-semitism within the Social Credit movement, hastened to equivocate: "That's not at all the party's view," he said, "at least not to my knowledge." In

227

ONE OF MY FIRST OFFICIAL ACTS AS PREMIER WILL BE TO WELCOME THE SOUTH AFRICAN AMBASSADOR TO MY OFFICE THEREBY MAKING ME THE ONLY CANADIAN PREMIER TO RECOGNIZE THE WHITE SOUTH AFRICAN GOVERNMENT — AND AS TO THE SILLY TRADE EMBARGO ADVOCATED BY THE U.N., CANADIAN GOVERNMENT, BISHOP TUTU AND THE LIKE, SELLING A LITTLE B.C. LUMBER TO "DESE WHITE BOYS DOWN DER" (HA, HA, HA,) MAY IMPROVE HOUSING FOR BLACK PEOPLE! — AH, HERE HE IS...

HA, HA, HA, HA, HA!

UNGAWA! HA, HA, HA, HA, HA...

...AS FOR THE 10,000 CASES OF SOUTH AFRICAN WINE THE GENERAL — I MEAN THE *PREMIER* — JUST PURCHASED, HE'S SUGGESTED WE USE THE AUSPICE OF "*PUBLIC DEMAND*" AS THE REASON, AND OH, YEAH... HE DECIDED TO GO AHEAD ON THE PLAN TO CHANGE THE NAME OF THE COUNTRY — I MEAN, *PROVINCE* — FROM "BRITISH COLUMBIA" TO THE NEW "*BAZOO COLUMBIA*"

his speech to the meeting he attacked the banking system without mentioning any conspiracies.

It was not Vander Zalm's first appearance at a meeting of the national party. The B.C. Social Credit party has been careful not to disassociate itself from the national organization, even over the sensational trial of hate-mongering national Socred Jim Keegstra. There is a grassroots element reflected in the national faction that the provincial powerbase, from the time of W.A.C. Bennett, has never opposed.

That grassroots element is fear: the insecurity of a middle class unsure of itself while desiring political solutions that promise not to change anything; a frustrated middle class in which the extremists preoccupy themselves with conspiracy theories, while the moderates lull themselves into sleep with nightmares of welfare deadbeats eating away at the fabric of society. The A+B Theorem, oil dividends, homeowner grants, bond-burning, BCRIC shares, megaprojects and the "investment climate": these are the panaceas of the Social Credit movement, the effect of which is to quiet fear for a little time, while preserving a demonological view of the world.

As we go to press, the Social Credit "position" has taken flesh in the physical body of Bill Vander Zalm. In the tradition of his Social Credit forbears, he has promised his electorate nothing and implied everything: nothing will change, but everything will be O.K.

The story of Social Credit is a catalogue of Utopian error: the quick fix that fixes nothing; the struggle against bogeymen that don't exist; the paranoid dreams of an uncomfortable middle class. Again and again, its intellectual resources exhaust themselves, only to be beaten back into consciousness on the rocky shoals of paranoia.

Social Credit has opened many roads to Utopia; each has been closed by the dogs of reality. There remain, however, fantasy venues yet to exploited; among them: *Tourism*, with its syphylitic sea captains, and *Gambling,* with its free enterprise profits.

Strongman Bill Vander Zalm, the fantasy Premier, has already expressed his interest in the free enterprise potential of organized gambling: the next great Social Credit initiative may in fact be already aborning...

The Nevada Solution?...

BIBLIOGRAPHY

Barr, John J. *The Dynasty: The Rise and Fall of Social Credit in Alberta*, Mc-Clelland and Stewart, 1974

Colbourne, Maurice. *The Meaning of Social Credit*, Alberta Social Credit Board, 1933

Douglas, C.H. *Brief for the Prosecution*, K.R.B. Publications, 1945

Douglas, C.H. *Credit-Power and Democracy*, Cecil Palmer, 1942.

Douglas, C.H. *The Big Idea*, K.R.B. Publications, 1942

Douglas, C.H. *The Monopoly of Credit*, K.R.P. Publications, 3rd edition, 1958

Finlay, John L. *Social Credit: The English Origins*, McGill Queens, 1972

Holter, E.S. *The ABC of Social Credit*, Longman Green, 1934

Irving, John A. *The Social Credit Movement in Alberta*, University of Toronto Press, 1959

Keene, Roger. *Conversations With W.A.C. Bennett*, Methuen, 1980

Lipset, Seymour. *Political Man*, Vantage, 1965

Magnusson, Warren, et al. *The New Reality*, New Star Books, 1984

Martin, Robin. *Pillars of Profit*, McClelland and Stewart, 1973

Mitchell, David J. *W.A.C. Bennett and the Rise of British Columbia*, Douglas & Mcintyre, 1983

Nichols, H.E. *Alberta's Fight for Freedom*, Alberta Social Credit League, 1963

Persky, Stan. *Bennett II*, New Star Books, 1983

Persky, Stan. *Son of Socred*, New Star Books, 1979.

Pound, E.L. *Social Credit: an Impact*, Peter Russell (reprint), 1951

Sanford, Thomas M. *Politics of Protest*, thesis, University of California, 1961

Social Credit Secretariat, *Elements of Social Credit*, K.R.P. Publications, 1946

Twigg, Alan. *Vander Zalm: from Immigrant to Premier*, Harbour Publishing, 1986

Wachtel, Eleanor, and Robert Anderson, eds. *The Expo Story*, Harbour Publishing, 1986

Born June 1949, has survived a childhood under Social Credit, and continues to persist under the present regime. He has illustrated four books of fiction (2 of them his own) and written three books of poetry, the most recent of which (1986) is *Under the Shadow of Thy Wings.* He is also the author/editor of Rough Beast Comix, which appear from time to time.

JOHN THOMAS OSBORNE

Born September 1947, shares the same background as his co-author. He has been an editor and publisher of literary and political books for fifteen years, the last few of which he has passed in front of a computer screen.

JAMES STEPHEN OSBORNE